BODY · MIND
BALANCING

ALSO BY OSHO

INSIGHTS FOR A NEW WAY OF LIVING SERIES

Awareness: The Key to Living in Balance
Courage: The Joy of Living Dangerously
Creativity: Unleashing the Forces Within
Freedom: The Courage to Be Yourself
Intelligence: The Creative Response to Now
Intimacy: Trusting Oneself and the Other
Intuition: Knowing Beyond Logic
Joy: The Happiness That Comes from Within
Maturity: The Responsibility of Being Oneself

OTHER BOOKS

Autobiography of a Spiritually Incorrect Mystic
The Book of Secrets
Pharmacy for the Soul
India My Love: A Spiritual Journey
Love, Freedom, and Aloneness
Meditation: The First and Last Freedom
Sex Matters
Your Answers Questioned
Art of Tea
Osho Transformation Tarot
Osho Zen Tarot
Tao: The Pathless Path
Zen: The Path of Paradox
Yoga: The Science of the Soul
Tarot in the Spirit of Zen

AUDIO

Book of Secrets: Keys to Love and Meditation
Osho Meditations on Buddhism
Osho Meditations on Sufism
Osho Meditations on Tantra
Osho Meditations on Tao
Osho Meditations on Yoga
Osho Meditations on Zen

BODY · MIND
BALANCING

USING YOUR MIND TO
HEAL YOUR BODY

OSHO

ST. MARTIN'S GRIFFIN

NEW YORK

NOTE TO READER

Any advice or teachings given in this book are not intended to replace the services of your physician, psychotherapist, or psychiatrist. Nor is the book meant to provide an alternative to professional medical treatment. This book offers no medical diagnosis of or treatment for any specific medical or psychological problems you may have. Some of the meditations include strenuous physical activity—if you have any reason to be concerned about the effects of such activity on your health, you should consult your physician before trying these meditations.

BODY MIND BALANCING. Copyright © 2003 by Osho International Foundation, Switzerland. www.osho.com. Copyright of the audio process © and (P) 2003 Osho International Foundation. All rights reserved. Printed in the United States of America. For information address St. Martin's Press, 175 Fifth Avenue, New York, N.Y. 10010.

This title is a special selection of excerpts taken from different works by Osho. The guided meditation process has been created by Osho.

Special thanks to the many friends who contributed to the production of the audio, "Reminding Yourself of the Forgotten Language of Talking to Your BodyMind," including Veet Marco for composing and playing the intuitive and supportive music for this process, Anando Hefley for the translation and recording of the English-language version, and Antar Alok for production and sound engineering.

OSHO is a registered trademark of Osho International Foundation, used with permission.

Book design by Ellen Cipriano

ISBN 0-312-33444-3
EAN 978-0312-33444-4

The body is the visible soul, and the soul is the invisible body. The body and soul are not divided anywhere, they are parts of each other, they are parts of one whole. You have to accept the body, you have to love the body, you have to respect the body, you have to be grateful to your body. . . .

The body is the most complex mechanism in existence— it is simply marvelous!

And blessed are those who marvel.

Begin the feeling of wonder with your own body, because that is the closest to you. The closest nature has approached to you, the closest existence has come to you, is through the body. In your body is the water of the oceans, in your body is the fire of the stars and the suns, in your body is the air, your body is made of earth.

Osho

CONTENTS

FOREWORD

The body is the visible soul, and the soul is the invisible body. The body and soul are not divided anywhere, they are parts of each other, they are parts of one whole. You have to accept the body, you have to love the body, you have to respect the body, you have to be grateful to your body. . . .

The body is the most complex mechanism in existence—it is simply marvelous!

And blessed are those who marvel.

Begin the feeling of wonder with your own body, because that is the closest to you.

The closest nature has approached to you, the closest existence has come to you, is through the body. In your body is the water of the oceans, in your body is the fire of the stars and the suns, in your body is the air, your body is made of earth. Your body represents the whole of existence, all the elements. And what a transformation! What a metamorphosis! Look at the earth, and then look at your body, what a transformation, and you have never marveled about it! Dust has become divine—what greater mystery is possible? What greater miracles are you waiting for? And you see the miracle happening every day. Out of the mud comes the lotus . . . and out of the dust has arisen our beautiful body.

.   .   .

A totally new kind of education is needed in the world where fundamentally everybody is introduced into the silences of the heart—in other words, into meditation—and where everybody has to be prepared to be compassionate to his or her own body. Because unless you are compassionate to your own body, you cannot be compassionate to any other body. It is a living organism, and it has done no harm to you. It has been continuously in service since you were conceived and will be until your death. It will do everything that you would like to do, even the impossible, and it will not be disobedient to you.

It is inconceivable to create a mechanism that is so obedient and so wise. If you become aware of all the functions of your body, you will be surprised. You have never thought about what your body has been doing. It is so miraculous, so mysterious. But you have never looked into it. You have never bothered to be acquainted with your own body and you pretend to love other people? You cannot, because those other people also appear to you as bodies.

The body is the greatest mystery in the whole of existence. This mystery needs to be loved, its mysteries and its functioning to be intimately inquired into. Religions have unfortunately been absolutely against the body. But that gives a clue, a definite indication that if a person learns the wisdom of the body and the mystery of the body, he will never bother about the priest or about God. He will have found the greatest mystery within himself, and within the mystery of the body is the very shrine of your consciousness.

Once you have become aware of your consciousness, of your being, there is no God above you. Only such a person can be respectful toward other human beings, toward other living beings, because they all are as mysterious as he himself is—different expressions, varieties, which make life richer. And once a person has found consciousness within, that person has found the key to the ultimate.

Any education that does not teach you to love your body does not teach you to be compassionate to your body, does not teach you how to enter into its mysteries, and will not be able to teach you how to enter into your own consciousness. The body is the door—the body is the stepping-stone, and any education that does not touch the subject of the body and consciousness is not only incomplete, it is also harmful because it will go on being destructive. It is only the flowering of consciousness within you that prevents you from being destructive. And that consciousness gives you a tremendous urge to create—to create more beauty in the world, to create more comfort in the world.

Man needs a better body, a healthier body. Man needs a more conscious, alert being.

Man needs all kinds of comforts and luxuries that existence is ready to deliver.

Existence is ready to give you paradise here now, but you go on postponing it—always to after death.

In Sri Lanka one great mystic was dying. He was revered by thousands of people and they gathered around him. He opened his eyes: just a few more breaths would he take on this shore, and then he would be gone, and gone forever. Everybody was eager to listen to his last words.

The old man said, "I have been teaching you for my whole life about blissfulness, ecstasy, meditativeness. Now I am going to the other shore. I will not be available anymore. You have listened to me, but you have never practiced what I have been telling you. You have always been postponing. But now there is no point in postponing, I am going. Is anyone ready to go with me?"

There was a great, pin-drop silence. People looked at each other, thinking, "Perhaps this man, who has been a disciple for forty years . . . *he* may be ready." But that man was just looking at the others—nobody was standing up. Just from the very back of the room, a man raised his hand. The mystic thought, "At least, one person is courageous enough."

But that man said, "Please let me make it clear to you why I am not standing up, I have only raised my hand. I want to know how to reach to the other shore, because today of course I am not ready. There are many things still not done. A guest has come, my young son is getting married, and on this day I cannot go. You say from the other shore, you cannot come back, but someday, one day certainly, I will come and meet you. If you can just explain to us once more— although you have been explaining for your whole life, just once more—how to reach the other shore? But please keep in mind that I am not ready to go right now. I just want to refresh my memory so that when the right time comes . . ."

That right time never comes.

It is not a story only about that poor man, it is the story of millions of people, of almost all. They are all waiting for the right moment, the right constellation of stars. . . . They are delving into astrology, going to the palmist, inquiring in different ways about what is going to happen tomorrow.

Tomorrow does not happen—it never has happened. It is simply a stupid strategy of postponement.

What happens is always today.

The right kind of education will teach you—and all people—

to live here now, to create a paradise out of this earth. It will teach you not to wait for death to come, and not to be miserable till death stops your misery. Let death find you dancing and joyous and loving.

If man can live his life as if he is already in paradise, death cannot take away anything from that experience. My approach is to teach you that this is the paradise, there is no paradise anywhere else, and no preparation is needed to be happy. No discipline is needed to be loving; just a little alertness, just a little wakefulness, just a little understanding. And if education cannot give you this little understanding, it is not education.

Doctors and scientists have now come to recognize what common sense has always told us—that there is a deep connection between body and mind, and it profoundly affects our overall physical health and sense of well-being. Researchers have found that nearly half our physical ailments are stress-related. And the "placebo effect"—where people get better just because they believe that a certain treatment or medicine is going to help them, even if they are only taking a sugar pill—is well documented.

"It's all in your head"—most of us have heard this expression more than once in our lives when we were complaining about this or that physical ailment or emotional difficulty . . . and although we might have denied it, we probably secretly suspected it was true. The problem is that just intellectually understanding that "it's all in my head" doesn't help. As Osho points out often in his talks, the thin layer of the conscious mind—the part that intellectually understands something—is only a tenth of our reality. The unconscious layers are far bigger, and when we're not in touch with them they can be far more powerful.

It is this set of relationships—between the conscious and unconscious layers of the mind, and their influence on the body and

our overall sense of well-being—that Osho addresses in a revolutionary technique he developed in 1989. It started as an experiment with his own body, when his shoulder was giving him a
great deal of pain. According to notes taken by his secretary at
the time, Osho told his shoulder to "drop the pain" and it did—
literally!—as the pain dropped from the shoulder first into the
arm, and then the leg. But he kept on experimenting, and in-
vited others also to experiment with a technique of talking to
the body and asking it to drop pain, that it was no longer needed
and once gone there was no need to bring it back. Over the next
few days and weeks, "Reminding Yourself of the Forgotten Language of Talking to the BodyMind" was born. It is now offered as
a seven-day series of one-hour sessions at the Osho Meditation
Resort in Pune, India, and offered around the world by individuals who have been trained in the process.

With the publication of this book-and-CD package, this process becomes available to individuals who can practice it on their
own, and health professionals and counselors who can recommend it to their clients.

The book has been created using a variety of selections from
talks by Osho, and begins by looking at the ideas we have about
the body and our relationship to it that we may not be aware of.
Almost everyone has been brought up with life-negative attitudes
and conditionings against the body. And well-meaning attempts
by parents and teachers to "civilize" children and help them to be
accepted into society often end up repressing their natural exu-
berance and vitality, the sharpness of their senses, and their cu-
riosity about their own bodies.

As adults we can't do anything to change our own history
and upbringing—but we can become aware of the hidden elements of that upbringing, and how they have affected us. The
magic is that in the very process of becoming aware, previously

unconscious attitudes begin to lose their power over us and we can begin to make new and more life-affirmative choices for ourselves. Once this new foundation is established, we find that we become more aware of the body and its real needs, more grateful and appreciative of its miraculous workings on our behalf, and better able to work with it, not against it, to achieve the goals we set for ourselves.

Physical health and psychological well-being are deeply related and interdependent. *Body Mind Balancing* provides both the conscious understanding and the practical tools that are needed to support this partnership of body and mind. See the last chapter of the book for specific guidance about how the guided meditation CD is to be used.

Carol Neiman, Editor

CHAPTER ONE

The Intelligence
of the Body

Western medical science has viewed man as a separate unit—apart from nature. That is one of the gravest errors that has been committed. Man is part of nature; his health is nothing but being at ease with nature.

Western medicine takes a mechanical view of man, so wherever mechanics can be successful, it is successful. But man is not a machine; man is an organic unity, and man needs not just treatment of the part that is sick. The sick part is only a symptom that the whole organism is going through difficulties. The sick part is only visible because it is the weakest.

You treat the sick part, and you seem successful . . . but then somewhere else the disease appears. You have only prevented the disease from expressing itself through the sick part; you have made it stronger. But you do not understand that man is a whole: either he is sick or he is healthy, there is no in-between. Man should be viewed as a whole organism.

It is fundamental to understand that the body is always ready to listen to you—but you have never talked with it, you have never communicated with it at all. You have been in it, you have used it, but you have never thanked it. It serves you, and serves you as intelligently as possible.

Nature knows that it is more intelligent than you are, because all the important things in the body have not been left to you, they have been given to the body. For example, breathing, or the heartbeat, or the blood circulating, or the digestion of the food—they have not been left up to you; otherwise you would have been in a mess long before. If breathing had been left to you, you would have died. There would be no possibility of your continuing to live because you can forget to breathe at any moment. If you fight with someone, you could forget to breathe. When you sleep at night, you could forget to make your heart beat. How would you remember? And do you know how much work your digestive system is doing? You go on swallowing things and you think you are doing a great job, that swallowing can be done by anybody.

In World War II it happened that one man got a bullet through his throat. He didn't die, but he could not eat or drink from the throat, the whole passage had to be closed. And the doctors made a small passage by the side of his stomach, with a pipe coming out, and he had to put the food in the pipe, but there was no joy. Even when he was putting in ice cream . . . he was very angry.

He said, "This is . . . I don't taste anything."

Then one doctor suggested, "Do it this way. First you taste the food, then insert into the pipe." And that he did for forty years. He would first chew and enjoy and then put it in the pipe. The pipe is just as good, because in your body too it is just a pipe and nothing else, it is just hidden behind skin. This unfortunate man's was just open. And it was better than yours because it could be cleaned and everything.

The whole digestive system is doing miracles. Scientists say that if each of us had to do everything that the small digestive system is doing we would need a big factory to turn food into blood, to sort out all elements, and to send those elements that are needed to certain places. A few elements are needed in the brain, and they have to be sent through the bloodstream to the brain. Others are needed elsewhere—to the eyes, to the ears, to the bones, or to the skin—and the body does it all perfectly for seventy, eighty, ninety years—but you don't see its wisdom.

THE WISDOM OF THE BODY

You have heard about alchemists who tried to transform base metals into gold. Your body does far better—it transforms all kinds of crap that you go on throwing inside into blood, into bone. And not only into blood and bone: it also turns that crap into nourishment for your brain. Out of your ice cream and Coca-Cola, it makes your brain, a brain that can create a Rutherford, an Albert Einstein, a Buddha, a Zarathustra, a Lao Tzu. Just see the miracle!

A brain is such a small thing, enclosed in a small skull. . . . A single brain can contain all the libraries of the world. Its capacity is almost infinite. It is the greatest memory system. If you want to make a computer of the same capacity you will need miles of space to make that computer function. And although science has developed so far, it has not been able to transform ice cream into blood. Scientists have been trying, but they cannot find the clue needed to transform ice cream into blood; make a brain out of ice cream! Perhaps it may never happen. Or even if it does, it will happen through the brain; it will be again a miracle of the brain.

TALK TO THE BODY

Once you start communicating with your body, things become very easy. The body need not be forced, it can be persuaded. One need not fight with the body—that's ugly, violent, aggressive, and any sort of conflict is going to create more and more tension. So you need not be in any conflict—let comfort be the rule. And the body is such a beautiful gift from God that to fight with it is to deny God Himself. It is a shrine . . . we are enshrined in it; it is a temple. We exist in it and we have to take every care of it—it is our responsibility.

It will look a little absurd in the beginning because we have never been taught to talk to our own body—but miracles can happen through it. They are already happening without our knowing it. When I speak to you, my hand follows in a gesture. I am talking to you—it is my mind that is communicating something to you. My body is following it. The body is en rapport with the mind.

When you want to raise the hand, you have to do nothing— you simply raise it. Just the idea that you want to raise it and the body follows; it is a miracle. In fact, biology or physiology has not yet been able to explain how it happens. Because an idea is an idea; you want to raise your hand—this is an idea. How does this idea become transformed into a physical message to the hand? And it does not take any length of time at all—just a split second; sometimes without any time gap.

For example, I am talking to you and my hand will go on collaborating; there is no time gap. It is as if the body is running parallel to the mind. It is very sensitive—you should learn how to talk to your body, and then many things can be done.

LISTEN TO THE BODY

Follow the body. Never in any way try to dominate the body. The body is your foundation. Once you have started understanding your body, 99 percent of your miseries will simply disappear.

But you don't listen—up to now. The body says, "Stop! Don't eat!" You go on eating; you listen to the mind. The mind says, "It is very tasty, delicious. A little more." You don't listen to the body. The body is feeling nauseous, the stomach is saying, "Stop! Enough is enough! I am tired!" but the mind says, "Look at the taste . . . a little bit more." You go on listening to the mind. If you listen to the body, 99 percent of your problems will simply disappear, and the remaining one percent will be just accidents, not really problems.

But from very early childhood we have been distracted from the body, we have been taken away from the body. The child is crying because he is hungry and the mother is looking at the clock because the doctor says that only after three hours is the child to be given milk. She is not looking at the child. The child is the real clock to look at, but she goes on looking at the clock. She listens to the doctor, but the child is crying and is asking for food, and the child needs food right now. If he is not given food right now you have distracted him from the body. Instead of giving him food you give him a pacifier. Now you are cheating and deceiving. You are giving something false, plastic, and you are trying to distract and destroy the child's sensitivity to his body. The wisdom of the body is not allowed to have its say; the mind enters in instead. The child is pacified by the pacifier and he falls asleep. Now the clock says three hours are over and you have to give the milk to the child. But now the child is fast asleep, and his body is sleeping; you wake him up, because the doctor says the milk has to be given now. You again destroy his rhythm. Slowly, slowly you disturb his whole being. The moment comes when he has lost all track of his body. He does not know what his body wants—he does not know whether his body wants to eat or not; whether the body wants to make love or not. Everything is manipulated by something from the outside. He looks at a *Playboy* magazine and feels like making love. Now this is stupid; this is the mind sending signals. The love cannot be very great; it will be just a sneeze, nothing else, an unburdening. It is not love at all. How can love

happen through the mind? Mind knows nothing of love. It becomes a duty. You have a wife, you have a husband, you have to
make love—it becomes a duty. Dutifully, religiously, every night,
you make love. Now the spontaneity is not there. And then you
are worried because you start feeling it is not fulfilling you. Then
you start looking for some other woman. You start thinking logi-
cally, "Maybe this woman is not the right woman for me. Maybe
she is not my soulmate. Maybe she is not made for me. I am not
made for her, because she's not turning me on."

The woman is not the problem, the man is not the problem:
you are not in the body, she is not in the body. If people were in
their bodies, nobody would miss that beauty called orgasm. If
people were in their bodies, they would know God's first glimpses
through their orgasmic experiences.

Listen to your body, follow the body. Mind is foolish; body is
wise. And if you have gone deep into the body, in those very
depths you will find your soul. The soul is hidden in the depths of
the body.

THE BODY IS A MIRACLE

It is tremendously beautiful, and tremendously complex. There
is nothing so complex, so subtle as the body. You don't know
anything about it. You have only looked at it in the mirror. You
have never looked at it from the within; otherwise it is a universe
in itself. That's what the mystics have always been saying: that the
body is a miniature universe. If you see it from the inside, it is so
vast—millions and millions of cells, and each cell alive with its
own life, and each cell functioning in such an intelligent manner
that it seems almost incredible, impossible, unbelievable.

You eat food, and the body transforms it into blood, bones, marrow. You eat food, and the body transforms it into consciousness, thought. A miracle is happening every moment. And each cell functions so systematically, in such an orderly way, with such an inner discipline, that it seems almost impossible—millions of cells. Seventy million cells are there in your single body—seventy million souls. Each cell has its own soul. And how well they function! They function with such coherence, in such rhythm and harmony. And the same cells become the eyes and the same cells become the skin and the same cells become your liver and your heart and your marrow and your mind and your brain. The same cells specialize—then they become specialized cells—but they are the same cells. And how well they move, and how subtly and silently they work.

Penetrate into it, go deep into the mystery of it. Because there you are rooted. The body is your earth; you are rooted in the body. Your consciousness is like a tree in the body. Your thoughts are like fruits. Your meditations are like flowers. But you are rooted in the body; the body supports it. The body supports everything that you are doing. You love; the body supports you. You hate; the body supports you. You want to kill somebody; the body supports you. You want to protect somebody; the body supports you. In compassion, in love, in anger, in hate—in every way—the body supports you. You are rooted in the body; you are nourished by the body. Even when you start realizing who you are, the body supports you.

The body is your friend; it is not your enemy. Listen to its language, decode its language, and by and by, as you enter into the book of the body and you turn its pages, you will become aware of the whole mystery of life. In condensed form, it is in your body. Magnified a millionfold, it is all over the world.

THE BODY HAS ALL THE MYSTERIES

The body has all the mysteries, all the mysteries that the whole universe has; it is a miniature universe. The difference between the body and the universe is only one of quantity. Just as a single atom has all the secrets of matter, the body has all the secrets of the universe. One need not go to search for any secrets outside, one has just to go inward.

And the body has to be taken care of. One should not be against it, one should not condemn it. If you condemn it, you have already condemned God, because in the deepest recess of the body God resides. God has chosen this house of the body to live in. Respect your body, love your body, care about your body.

The so-called religions have created much antagonism between man and his body. It is true that you are not the body, but that doesn't mean that you have to be against it; the body is your friend. The body can take you to hell, the body can take you to heaven too. It is simply a vehicle. It is neutral: wherever you want to go, it is ready. It is a mechanism of immense complexity, beauty, order. The more one understands one's body, the more one feels awe. Then what to say about the whole universe? Even this small body is so much of a miracle; therefore I call the body the temple of the divine.

And once your attitude toward the body changes it becomes easier to go in, because the body becomes open to you. It allows you to come in; it starts revealing its secrets to you. That's how all the secrets of Yoga were first known. That's how all the secrets of Tao were first known. Yoga didn't arise out of dissecting dead bodies. Modern medical science is based on dead bodies and their dissection. It has something basically wrong with it. It has not yet been able to know the living body. To dissect a dead body is one thing, to know something about it is another thing, but to know something about a living body is totally different. Modern science has no way of knowing about the living body. The only way it knows is to butcher it, to cut it open, but the moment you cut it, it is no longer the same phenomenon. To understand a flower on the stem, on the tree, is one thing; to cut it and dissect it is totally another. It is no longer the same phenomenon; its quality is different.

Albert Einstein the man has some qualities that the corpse will not have, cannot have. A poet dies—the body is there but where is the poetry? A genius dies—the body is there but where is the genius? The body of the idiot and the body of the genius are the same. You will not be able to know by dissecting the body whether it belonged to a genius or an idiot, whether it belonged to a mystic or to someone who was never aware of anything mysterious in life. It will be impossible because you are simply looking into the house, and the being who lived there is no more there. You are simply studying the cage and the bird has gone; and to study the cage is not to study the bird. But still, the body contains the divine in it.

The real way is to go within yourself and watch your own body from there, from the interiormost of your being. Then it is a tremendous joy . . . just to see its functioning, its ticking. It is the greatest miracle that has happened in the universe.

BODY-MIND CONNECTIONS

Most problems are psychosomatic because the body and the mind are not two separate things. The mind is the inner part of the body, and the body is the outer part of the mind, so anything can start in the body and can enter into the mind, or vice versa: it can start in the mind and enter into the body. There is no division; there is no watertight compartment.

So most problems have two edges to them: they can be tackled through the mind and through the body. And up to now this has been the practice in the world: a few people believe that all problems are of the body—the physiologists, the Pavlovians, the behaviorists . . . They treat the body, and of course in 50 percent of the cases they succeed. And they hope that as science grows they will be succeeding more, but they will never succeed beyond 50 percent; it has nothing to do with the growth of science.

Then there are those who think that all problems are of the mind—which is as wrong as the first premise. Christian Scientists and hypnotists and mesmerists; they all think problems are of the mind . . . as do psychotherapists. They also succeed in 50 percent of the cases; they, too, think that sooner or later they will succeed more and more. That is nonsense. They cannot succeed beyond 50 percent; that is the limit.

My own understanding is that each problem has to be tackled from both sides at the same time; it has to be attacked from both perspectives, a double-fronted attack. Then man can be cured 100 percent. Whenever science becomes perfect it will work both ways.

The first place to start is the body, because the body is the portal to the mind—the porch. And because the body is gross, it is easily manipulatable. First the body has to be freed of all its accumulated structures and at the same time your mind has to be inspired so that it can start moving upwards and can start dropping all the loads that keep it down.

YOUR MIND AND YOUR BODY
ARE NOT TWO SEPARATE THINGS

Remember that always. Do not say, "physiological process" and "mental process." They are not two processes—just two parts of one whole. Whatsoever you do physiologically affects the mind. Whatsoever you do psychologically affects the body. They are not two, they are one.

You can say that the body is a solid state of the same energy and the mind is a liquid state of the same energy—of the same energy! So no matter what you are doing physiologically, do not think that this is just physiological. Do not wonder how it is going to help any transformation in the mind. If you take alcohol, what happens to your mind? Alcohol is taken in the body, not in the mind, but what happens to the mind? If you take LSD, it goes into the body, not into the mind, but what happens to the mind?

Or if you go on a fast, fasting is done by the body, but what happens to the mind? Or from the other end: if you think sexual thoughts, what happens to your body? The body is affected immediately. In your mind you think of a sex object and your body starts getting ready.

There was a theory by William James in the first part of the 20th century that apparently looked very absurd, but in a sense it was right. He and another scientist named Lange elucidated what became known as the James-Lange theory. Ordinarily, we say you are afraid and that is why you escape and run away, or you are angry and that is why your eyes get red and you start beating your enemy. But James and Lange proposed quite the contrary. They said that because you run away, that is why you feel fear; and because your eyes get red and you start beating your enemy, you feel anger. They proposed that it is just the opposite. They said that if this is not so, then we want to see even one instance of anger when the eyes are not red and the body is not affected and one is simply angry. Do not allow your body to be affected and try to be angry—then you will know that you cannot be angry.

In Japan they teach their children a very simple method of controlling anger. They say, whenever you feel angry, do not do anything with the anger, just start taking deep breaths. Try it, and you will not be able to get angry. Why? Just because you take deep breaths, why can you not get angry? It becomes impossible to get angry. There are two reasons. You start taking deep breaths, but anger needs a particular rhythm of breathing, and without that rhythm anger is not possible. A particular rhythm in breathing or chaotic breathing is needed for anger to exist.

If you start taking deep breaths, it is impossible for the anger to come out. If you are consciously taking deep breaths, then the anger cannot express itself. Anger requires a different breathing pattern. You need not do it; the anger will do it itself. With deep breathing, you cannot be angry.

And secondly, your mind shifts. When you feel angry and you start to take deep breaths, your mind shifts from anger to breathing. The body is not in a state to be angry, and the mind has shifted its concentration toward something else. Then it is difficult to be angry. That is why the Japanese are the most controlled people on earth. It is just a training from childhood.

It is difficult anywhere else to find such an incident, but in Japan it happens even today. It is happening less and less because Japan is becoming less and less Japanese. It is becoming more and more Westernized, and the traditional methods and ways are becoming lost. But it was happening, and it still happens today.

One of my friends was there in Kyoto, and he wrote me a letter saying, "I have seen such a beautiful phenomenon today that I want to write about it to you. And when I come back, I will want to understand how it is possible. One man was struck by a car. He fell down, stood up, thanked the driver, and went away—he thanked the driver!"

In Japan it is not difficult. He must have taken a few deep breaths, and then it was possible. You are transformed into a different attitude, and you can thank even a person who was just going to kill you, or who has already tried to kill you.

Physiological processes and psychological processes are not two separate things, they are one, and you can start from either pole to affect and change the other.

TREATING MAN AS A WHOLE

In a better world every person whose profession is to treat the body will meditate. And when the body is suffering, there must be something behind it, because everything is interwoven. So no person can be treated just by treating his body—his totality has to be treated. But to look into his totality, you have to look into your own totality.

Every physician should be a meditator, otherwise he will never be a real physician. He may have degrees, and he may have a license to practice medicine, but to me he is a quack because he does not know the whole person, so he will treat just symptoms.

Somebody has a certain symptom, a migraine or a headache—you can treat it, but you don't look deep inside as to why the person has the migraine in the first place. Maybe she is too burdened, worried, depressed. Maybe she has shrunken so much inside that it hurts. Maybe he is thinking too much and is not relaxing his mind at all. So you can treat the symptom, and you can force the symptom to disappear through poisons and medicines.

But it will appear somewhere else, because the root cause has not been touched at all.

Symptoms should not be treated, but persons should. And a person is organic, total. Sometimes it happens that the disease may be in the feet and the root cause may be in the head. Sometimes the root cause may be in the head, and the disease may be in the feet. Because the human being is one . . . absolutely connected! Nothing is disconnected in the human being. And not only is the body connected in itself, the body is connected with the mind, and then body and mind—soma and psyche—both are connected to a transcendental soul.

CHAPTER TWO

Decoding Life-Negative Conditioning

*T*he only duty you have is to be happy. Make it a religion to be happy. If you are not happy, then whatsoever you are doing, something must be wrong and some drastic change is needed. Let happiness decide.

I am a hedonist. And happiness is the only criterion man has.

So always look at what happens when you do something: if you become peaceful or restful at home, relaxed, it is right. This is the criterion; nothing else is the criterion. What is right for you may not be right for somebody else; remember that too. Because what is easy for you may not be easy for somebody else; something else may be easy for him. So there can be no universal law about it. Every individual has to work it out for himself. What is easy for you?

WHY WE CHOOSE TO BE UNHAPPY

This is one of the most complex human problems. It has to be considered very deeply, and it is not theoretical—it concerns you. This is how everybody is behaving—always choosing the wrong way, always choosing to be sad, depressed, miserable. There must be profound reasons for it, and there are.

First, the way human beings are brought up plays a very

definite role. If you are unhappy, you gain something from it; you always gain. If you are happy, you always lose.

From the very beginning an alert child senses the distinction. Whenever he is unhappy, everybody is sympathetic toward him, he gains sympathy. Everybody tries to be loving toward him, he gains love. And even more than that whenever he is unhappy everybody is attentive toward him, he gains attention. Attention works like food for the ego, a very alcoholic stimulant. It gives you energy; you feel you are somebody. Hence so much need, so much desire to get attention.

If everybody is looking at you, you become important. If nobody is looking at you, you feel as if you are not there, you are no more, you are a non-being. People looking at you, people caring about you gives you energy.

The ego exists in relationship. The more people pay attention to you, the more you gain ego. If nobody looks at you, the ego dissolves. If everybody has completely forgotten you, how can the ego exist? How can you feel that you are? Hence the need for societies, associations, clubs. All over the world clubs exist—Rotary, Lions, Masonic Lodges—millions of clubs and societies. These societies and clubs exist only to give attention to people who cannot get attention in other ways.

From the very beginning a child learns the politics. The politics are: look miserable, then you get sympathy, then everybody is attentive. Look ill—you become important. An ill child becomes dictatorial; the whole family has to follow him—whatever he says is the rule.

When he is happy, nobody listens to him. When he is healthy, nobody cares about him. When he is perfect, nobody is attentive. From the very beginning we start choosing the miserable, the sad, the pessimistic, the darker side of life. That's one reality.

A second thing related to it is: whenever you are happy,

whenever you are joyful, whenever you feel ecstatic and blissful, everybody is jealous of you. Jealousy means that everybody is antagonistic, nobody is friendly; at that moment, everybody is an enemy. So you have learned not to be so ecstatic that everybody becomes inimical toward you—not to show your bliss, not to laugh.

Look at people when they laugh. They laugh very calculatingly. It is not a belly-laugh, it is not coming from the very depth of their being. They first look at you, then they judge . . . and then they laugh. And they laugh to a particular extent, the extent you will tolerate, the extent which will not be taken amiss, the extent where nobody will become jealous.

Even our smiles are political. Laughter has disappeared, bliss has become absolutely unknown, and to be ecstatic is almost impossible because it is not allowed. If you are miserable, nobody will think you are mad. If you are ecstatic and dancing, everybody will think you are mad. Dance is rejected, singing is not accepted. A blissful man—we think something has gone wrong if we see one.

What type of society is this? If someone is miserable, everything is okay; he fits because the whole society is miserable, more or less. He is a member, he belongs to us. If somebody becomes ecstatic, we think he has gone berserk, insane. He doesn't belong to us—and we feel jealous.

Because of jealousy we condemn him. Because of jealousy we will try in every way to put him back to his old state. We call that old state normality. Psychoanalysts will help, psychiatrists will help to bring that man to the normal misery.

Society cannot allow ecstasy. Ecstasy is the greatest revolution. I repeat it: ecstasy is the greatest revolution. If people become ecstatic, the whole society will have to change, because this society is based on misery.

If people are blissful, you cannot lead them to war—to

Vietnam, or to Egypt, or to Israel. No. Someone who is blissful will just laugh and say: This is nonsense!

If people are blissful, you cannot make them obsessed with money. They will not waste their whole lives just accumulating money. It will look like madness to them that a person is destroying his whole life, just exchanging his life for dead money, dying and accumulating money. And the money will be there when he is dead. This is absolute madness! But this madness cannot be seen unless you are ecstatic.

If people are ecstatic, then the whole pattern of this society will have to change. This society exists on misery. Misery is a great investment for this society. So we bring up children . . . from the very beginning we create a leaning toward misery. That's why they always choose misery.

In the morning everybody has a choice. And not only in the morning, every moment there is a choice to be miserable or to be happy. You always choose to be miserable because there is an investment. You always choose to be miserable because that has become a habit, a pattern; you have always done that. You have become efficient at doing it; it has become a track. The moment your mind has to choose, it immediately flows toward misery.

Misery seems to be downhill; ecstasy seems to be uphill. Ecstasy looks very difficult to reach—but it is not so. The real thing is quite the opposite: ecstasy is downhill, misery is uphill. Misery is a very difficult thing to achieve, but you have achieved it, you have done the impossible—because misery is so antinature. Nobody wants to be miserable and everybody IS miserable.

Society has done a great job. Education, culture, and the culturing agencies, parents, teachers—they have done a great job. They have made miserable creatures out of ecstatic creators. Every child is born ecstatic. Every child is born a god. And every man dies a madman.

This is your whole work—how to regain childhood, how to reclaim it. If you can become a child again, then there is no misery. I don't mean that for a child there are no moments of misery—there are. But still there is no misery. Try to understand this.

A child can become miserable, he can be unhappy, intensely unhappy in a moment, but he is so total in that unhappiness, he is so one with that unhappiness, that there is no division. The child separate from unhappiness does not exist. The child is not looking at his unhappiness separate, divided. The child *is* unhappiness—he is so involved in it. And when you become one with unhappiness, unhappiness is not unhappiness. If you become so one with it, even that has a beauty of its own.

So look at a child—an unspoilt child, I mean. If he is angry, then his whole energy becomes anger; nothing is left behind, nothing is reserved. He has moved and become anger; there is nobody manipulating and controlling the anger. There is no mind. The child has become anger—he is not angry, he has become the anger. And then see the beauty, the flowering of anger. The child never looks ugly—even in anger he looks beautiful. He just looks more intense, more vital, more alive—a volcano ready to erupt. Such a small child, such a great energy, such an atomic being—with the whole universe to explode.

And after this anger the child will be silent. After this anger the child will be very peaceful. After this anger the child will relax. We may think it is very miserable to be in that anger, but the child is not miserable—he has enjoyed it.

If you become one with anything you become blissful. If you separate yourself from anything, even if it is happiness, you will become miserable.

So this is the key. To be separate as an ego is the base of all misery; to be one, to be flowing, with whatever life brings to you, to be in it so intensely, so totally, that you are no more, you are lost, then everything is blissful.

The choice is there, but you have even become unaware of the choice. You have been choosing the wrong thing so continuously, it has become such a habit, that you simply choose it automatically. There is no choice left.

Become alert. Each moment when you are choosing to be miserable remember: this is your choice. Even this mindfulness will help, the alertness that this is my choice and I am responsible, and this is what I am doing to myself, this is my doing. Immediately you will feel a difference. The quality of mind will have changed. It will be easier for you to move towards happiness.

And once you know that this is your choice, then the whole thing has become a game. Then if you love to be miserable, be miserable, but remember that this is your choice and don't complain. There is nobody else responsible. This is your drama. If you like it this way, if you like the miserable way, if you want to pass through life in misery, then this is your choice, your game. You are playing it. Play it well!

Don't go and ask people how not to be miserable. That is absurd. Don't go and ask masters and gurus how to be happy. The so-called gurus exist because you are foolish. You create the misery, and then you go and ask others how to uncreate it. And you will go on creating misery because you are not alert to what you are doing. From this very moment try, try to be happy and blissful.

TWO WAYS TO LIVE

There are two ways to live, to be, to know: one is of effort, will, ego; the other is of no effort, no struggle, but being in a let-go with existence.

All the religions of the world have been teaching you the first way, to fight—fight against nature, fight against the world, fight against your own body, fight against the mind. Only then can you achieve the truth, the ultimate, the eternal. But it is enough proof that this will to power, this path of the ego, this fighting and war has utterly failed. In millions of years, very few people have achieved the ultimate experience of life, so few that they only prove the exception, they don't prove the rule.

I teach you the second way: don't go against the current of existence, go with it; it is not your enemy. Just as a person can try to go upstream, fighting with the river, soon he will be tired and he is not going to get anywhere. The river is vast and he is a small part.

In this vast existence, you are smaller than an atom. How can you fight against the whole? The very idea is unintelligent. And you are produced by the whole, so how can it be your enemy? Nature is your mother; it cannot be against you. Your body is your very life it cannot be antagonistic to you. It serves you in spite of your continuous fight with it. It serves you when you are awake, it serves you even when you are asleep. Who goes on breathing? You are fast asleep and snoring. Your body has its own wisdom. It continues to breathe, the heart continues to beat, the body goes on functioning without you. In fact, it functions better when you are not present. Your presence is always a disturbance, because your mind is conditioned by people who have told you to be against it.

I teach you to have a friendship with existence. I do not want you to renounce the world, because the world is yours, ours. Nothing that exists is against you. All that you have to learn is the art of living—not the art of renouncing, but the art of rejoicing. It is only a question of learning an art and you can change the poison into nectar.

On so many medicines you will find written the word poison,

but in the hands of a scientific expert the poison has become a medicine. It does not kill you; it saves you.

If you find that somewhere your body, nature, the world is against you, remember one thing: it must be your ignorance; it must be some wrong attitude. It must be that you don't know the art of living. You are unaware that existence cannot be against you. You are born out of it, you live in it, it has given everything to you and you are not even grateful. On the contrary, all religions have been teaching you to condemn it from the very beginning.

Any religion that teaches you condemnation of life is poisonous. It is antilife; it is in the service of death; it is not in the service of you, it is not in the service of existence. But why does the question arise?

All these religions went against nature. Why did they create a certain logic that unless you are against this world, you will never be able to achieve the other world, the higher one? Why did they make such a division between this world and that world? There is a reason for it.

If this world is not to be renounced but lived in its totality, then the priest is no longer needed. If this world has to be fought, renounced, you have to repress your natural instincts. Then of course, you are going to be in a sick state. Against nature you can never be healthy, you can never be whole. You will always be split and schizophrenic. Naturally, you will need somebody to guide you, somebody to help you—you will need the priest.

Naturally, when you are guilty, you go to the church, the mosque, the synagogue; you ask the priest, the minister, the rabbi to help you, because in your deep darkness—which they are responsible for creating—you are so helpless, you need somebody to protect you, somebody to help you, somebody to show you the light. You are in such desperate need that you don't ever think about whether the priest knows anything more than you do, or whether he is just a paid servant.

Your problem is basically to look within yourself, where you are. And if you are in misery, in suffering, in anxiety, in anguish; if you are missing something in life, if you are discontented, if you don't see any meaning anywhere and you are simply dragging yourself toward death . . .

The darkness goes on growing darker, every day death goes on coming nearer—is this the time to get into great theological problems? It is the time to change your being. You do not have much time.

And the methods that all the religions have been teaching to you are methods of fighting; they don't lead anywhere. They simply spoil your joys of life. They poison everything enjoyable in this life. They have created a sad humanity. I would like a humanity full of love and full of song and full of dance.

So I want it to be clearly understood that my method is the second one, and by the second method I mean you are not to fight the current and go upstream—that is stupid. You cannot fight because the current of nature is too big and too strong. The best way is to learn from a dead body. Dead people know a few secrets that living people don't know.

Living people drown, if they don't know how to swim. This is very strange because by the time they are dead, they surface again. When they were living, they went down; when they died, they came up. Certainly, the dead person knows something the living person does not. What happened? Why do the river and the ocean behave differently with the dead person? The dead person is in absolute let-go. He is not even swimming. He is not doing anything.

The best swimmer simply floats. The ultimate swimmer, like a dead body, just goes with the current, wherever the river leads—it always leads to the ocean. Every river leads to the ocean, so you need not be worried whether you are in a holy river or not. Holy or unholy, every river is destined to reach the ocean sooner or later. You just go on floating with the river. And this I call trust—trusting in existence that wherever it leads, it leads to the right path, to the right goal. It is not your enemy. Trust in nature that wherever it is taking you, there is your home.

If the whole of humanity learns relaxation rather than fighting, learns let-go rather than making arduous effort, there will be a great change in the quality of consciousness. Relaxed people, simply moving silently with the flow of the river, having no goals of their own, having no egos . . .

In such a relaxed floating you cannot have any ego. Ego needs effort—you have to do something. Ego is a doer, and by floating you have become a non-doer. In this inaction, you will be surprised how your anxieties and miseries start dropping away and how you start becoming contented with whatever existence gives to you.

Let me tell you about one Sufi mystic who was traveling.

Every evening he would thank existence: "You have done so much for me and I have not been able to repay it, and I will never be able to repay it." His disciples were a little disgusted, because sometimes life was so arduous.

The Sufi mystic was a rebellious person. It happened this time that for three days they had no food, because every village they passed refused them because they were not orthodox Mohammedans. They had joined a rebellious group of Sufis. The people wouldn't give them shelter for the night, so they were sleeping in the desert. They were hungry, they were thirsty, and it was now the third day. At the evening prayer, the mystic again said to existence, "I am so grateful.

You have been doing so much for us and we cannot ever re-pay it."

One of the disciples said, "This is too much. Now for three days please tell us what existence has done for us? For what are you thanking existence?"

The old man laughed. He said, "You are still not aware of what existence has done for us. These three days have been very significant for me. I was hungry, I was thirsty; we had no shelter; we were rejected, condemned. Stones were thrown at us, and I was watching within myself—no anger arose. I am thanking existence. Its gifts are invaluable. I can never repay them. Three days of hunger, three days of thirst, three days of no sleep, people throwing stones . . . and yet I have not felt any enmity, any anger, any hatred, any failure, any disappointment. It must be your mercy; it must be existence supporting me.

"These three days have revealed so many things to me which would not have been revealed if food had been given, reception had been given, shelter had been given, stones had not been thrown—and you are asking me for what I am thanking existence? I will thank existence even when I am dying, because even in death I know existence is going to reveal mysteries to me as it has been revealing them in life, because death is not the end but the very climax of life."

Learn to flow with existence so you don't have any guilt and any wounds. Don't fight with your body, or nature, or anything, so you are at peace and at home, calm and collected.

This will help you to become more alert, more aware, more conscious, which finally leads to the ocean of ultimate awakening—liberation.

THE BODY IS YOUR FRIEND

All the religions have been teaching you to fight against nature. Whatever is natural is condemned. All religions say that you have to manage to do something unnatural, only then can you get out of the imprisonment of biology, physiology, psychology, all the walls that surround you. But if you go on in harmony with your body, with your mind, with your heart, religions say you will never be able to go beyond yourself. That's where I oppose all religions. They have put a poisonous seed in your being, so you live in your body, but you don't love your body.

The body serves you for seventy, eighty, ninety, even a hundred years, and there is no other mechanism that science has been able to invent that can be compared to the body. Its complexities, the miracles that it goes on doing for you . . . and you don't even say thank you. You treat your body as your enemy, but your body is your friend.

It takes care of you in every possible way, while you are awake and while you are asleep. When you are asleep and a spider starts crawling on your leg, your leg throws it off without bothering you. The leg has a small brain of its own. So for small matters there is no need to go to the central system, to go to the brain—the leg can do that much on its own. If a mosquito is biting you, your hands move it or kill it, and your sleep is not disturbed. So while you sleep your body protects you and does things of which you are not generally aware. The hand is not supposed to have a brain, but certainly it has something that can only be called a very small brain. Perhaps every cell of your body has a small brain in it. And there are millions of cells in your body, millions of small brains, moving around, continuously taking care.

You go on eating all kinds of things without bothering to think about what happens when you swallow them. You don't ask your body whether its mechanism, its chemistry, will be able to digest what you are eating. But somehow your inner chemistry goes on working for almost a century. It has an automatic system that replaces parts which have gone wrong. It goes on expelling defective parts, creating new ones; and you do not have to do anything, it happens on its own. The body has a certain wisdom of its own.

Religions go on saying to you, "You have to fight always, you have to move against the current. Don't listen to the body—whatever it says, do just the opposite." Jainism says, "The body is hungry; let it be hungry. You starve it; it needs that treatment." It simply serves you without any payment from you, no salary, no facilities, and Jainism says to go against it. When your body wants to fall asleep, Jainism says you should try to remain awake.

This certainly gives you great ego power. When the body wants food, you say no. "No" has great power to it. You are the master. You reduce the body to a slave—not only to a slave, you force the body to keep its mouth shut: "Whatever I decide is going to be done; you are not to interfere."

Do not fight with your body. It is not your foe, it is your friend. It is nature's gift to you. It is part of nature. It is joined with nature in every possible way. You are connected to breathing; you are connected to the sunrays, to the fragrance of flowers, to the moonlight. You are connected to all; you are not a separate island. Drop that idea. You are part of this whole continent, and yet it has given you an individuality. This is what I call a miracle.

You are part and parcel of existence, yet you have an individuality. Existence has performed a miracle, has made possible something impossible.

Being in harmony with your body, you also will be in harmony with nature, with existence. So instead of going against the current, go with the current. Be in a let-go. Allow life to happen. Don't force anything, not even for the sake of some holy book, for the sake of some holy ideal. Never disturb your harmony.

Nothing is more valuable than to be harmonious, in accord with the whole.

Respect life, revere life. There is nothing more holy than life, nothing more divine than life. And life does not consist of big things. Those religious fools have been telling you to "Do big things," but life consists of small things. Their strategy is clear. They tell you, "Do big things, do something great, something that your name will be remembered for afterwards." And of course this appeals to the ego. The ego is the agent of the priest. All the churches and the synagogues and the temples have only one agent, and that is the ego. They don't use different agencies; there are none. There is only one agency, and that is the ego—do something great, something big.

I want to tell you that there is nothing big, nothing great. Life consists of very small things. So if you become interested in the so-called big things, you will be missing life.

Life consists of sipping a cup of tea, gossiping with a friend; going for a morning walk, but not going anywhere in particular, just for a walk, with no goal, no end, from any point you can turn back; cooking food for someone you love; cooking food for yourself, because you love your body too; washing your clothes, cleaning the floor, watering the garden—these small things, very small things. Saying hello to a stranger, which was not needed at all because there was no question of any business with the stranger. The man who can say hello to a stranger can also say hello to a flower, can also say hello to a tree, can sing a song to the birds. The birds sing every day and you have not considered at all with then, but some day you should return the call. Just small things, very small things . . .

Respect your life. Out of that respect you will start respecting life in others.

THE GHOST OF "OUGHT"

Our whole education—in the family, in society, in the school, in college, in the university—creates tension in us. And the fundamental tension is that you are not doing that which you "ought" to do.

This persists in your whole life; it follows you like a nightmare, it goes on haunting you. It will never leave you at rest; it will never allow you to relax. If you relax, it will say, "What are you doing? You are not supposed to relax; you should be doing something." If you are doing something, it will say, "What are you doing? You need some rest, it is a must, otherwise you will drive yourself crazy—you are already on the verge."

If you do something good, it will say, "You are a fool. Doing good is not going to pay, people will cheat you." If you do something bad, it will say, "What are you doing? You are preparing the way to hell, you will have to suffer for it." It will never leave you at rest; whatsoever you do, it will be there condemning you.

This condemner has been implanted in you. This is the greatest calamity that has befallen humanity. And unless we get rid of this condemner inside us we cannot be truly human, we cannot be truly joyous, and we cannot participate in the celebration that life is.

And now nobody can drop it except you. And this is not only your problem, it is the problem of almost every human being. Whatever country you are born in, whatever religion you belong to, it doesn't matter——Catholic, communist, Hindu, Muslim, Jaina, Buddhist, it does not matter to what kind of ideology you belong, the essential is the same. The essential is to create a split in you, so one part always condemns the other part. If you follow the first part, then the second part starts condemning you. You are in an inner conflict, a civil war.

This civil war has to be dropped, otherwise you will miss the whole beauty, the benediction of life. You will never be able to laugh to your heart's content, you will never be able to love, you will never be able to be total in anything. And it is only out of totality that one blooms, that the spring comes, and your life starts having color and music and poetry.

It is only out of totality that suddenly you feel the presence of God all around you. But the irony is that the split has been created by your so-called saints, priests, and churches. In fact, the priest has been the greatest enemy of God on the earth.

We have to get rid of all the priests; they are the root cause of human pathology. They have made everybody ill at ease; they have caused an epidemic of neurosis. And the neurosis has become so prevalent that we take it for granted. We think that this is all life is about, we think this is what life is——a suffering, a long, long, delayed suffering; a painful, agonizing existence; an autobiography of much ado about nothing.

And if we look at our so-called life, it seems so, because there is never a single flower, never a single song in the heart, never a ray of divine delight.

It is not surprising that intelligent people all over the world are asking what the meaning of life is. "Why should we go on living? Why are we so cowardly as to go on living? Why can't we gather a little courage and put a stop to all this nonsense? Why can't we commit suicide?"

Never before in the world were there so many people thinking that life is utterly meaningless. Why has this happened in this age? First, it has nothing to do with this age. For centuries, for at least five thousand years, the priests have been doing the harm. Now we have come to the ultimate crisis.

It is not our doing; we are victims. We are the victims of history. If man wants to become a little more conscious, the first thing to do is to burn all the history books. Forget the past; it was nightmarish. Start anew from ABC, as if Adam is born again. Start as if we are again in the garden of Eden, innocent, uncontaminated . . .

A man was looking for a good church to attend and found a small one in which the congregation was reading with the minister. They were saying, "We have left undone those things we ought to have done and we have done those things which we ought not to have done."

The man dropped into a seat and sighed with relief as he said to himself, "Thank goodness, I've found my crowd at last."

Do what your nature wants to do, do what your intrinsic qualities hanker to do. Don't listen to the scriptures, listen to your own heart; that is the only scripture I prescribe. Yes, listen very attentively, very consciously, and you will never be wrong. And if you listen to your own heart, you will never be divided. Listening to your own heart, you will start moving in the right direction, without ever thinking of what is right and what is wrong.

So the whole art for the new humanity will consist in the secret of listening to the heart consciously, alertly, attentively. And follow it through any means, and go wherever it takes you. Yes, sometimes it will take you into danger—but then remember, those dangers are needed to make you ripe. And sometimes it will take you astray—but remember again, those goings astray are part of growth. Many times you will fall. Rise up again, because this is how one gathers strength—by falling down and rising again. This is how one becomes integrated.

But don't follow rules imposed from the outside. No imposed rule can ever be right, because rules are invented by people who want to rule you. Yes, sometimes there have been great enlightened people in the world too—a Buddha, a Jesus, a Krishna, a Mohammed. They have not given the world rules, they have given their love. But sooner or later the disciples gather together and start drawing up codes of conduct. Once the master is gone, once the light is gone and they are in deep darkness, they start groping for certain rules to follow, because now the light in which they could have seen is no longer there. Now they will have to depend on rules.

What Jesus did was his own heart's whispering, and what Christians go on doing is not their own hearts' whispering. They are imitators—and the moment you imitate, you insult your humanity, you insult your God.

Never be an imitator; always be original. Don't become a carbon copy. But that's what is happening all over the world— carbon copies and more carbon copies.

Life is really a dance if you are an original—and you are meant to be an original. And no two men are alike, so my way of life can never become your way of life.

Imbibe the spirit, imbibe the silence of the master, learn his grace. Drink as much out of his being as possible, but don't imitate him. Imbibing his spirit, drinking his love, receiving his compassion, you will be able to listen to your own heart's whisperings. And they are whisperings. The heart speaks in a very still, small voice; it does not shout.

Forget all about what you have been told—"This is right and this is wrong." Life is not so fixed. The thing that is right today may be wrong tomorrow, the thing that is wrong this moment may be right the next. Life cannot be pigeonholed; you cannot label it so easily as "This is right and this is wrong." Life is not a chemist's shop where every bottle is labeled and you know what is what. Life is a mystery; one moment something fits and then it is right. Another moment, so much water has gone down the Ganges that it no longer fits and it is wrong.

What is my definition of right? That which is harmonious with existence is right, and that which is disharmonious with existence is wrong. You will have to be very alert each moment, because it has to be decided each moment afresh. You cannot depend on ready-made answers for what is right and what is wrong.

Life moves so fast; it is a dynamism, it is not static. It is not a stagnant pool, it is a Ganges, it goes on flowing. It is never the same for two consecutive moments. So one thing may be right this moment, and may not be right the next.

Then what to do? The only possible thing is to make people so aware that they themselves can decide how to respond to a changing life.

There is an old Zen story.

There were two temples, rivals. Both the masters— they must have been so-called masters, must have really been priests—were so much against each other that they told their followers never to look at the other temple.

Each of the priests had a boy to serve him, to go and fetch things for him, to go on errands. The priest of the first temple told his boy servant, "Never talk to the other boy. Those people are dangerous."

But boys are boys. One day they met on the road, and the boy from the first temple asked the other, "Where are you going?"

The other said, "Wherever the wind takes me." He must have been listening to great Zen things in the temple because he said, "Wherever the wind takes me." A great statement, pure Tao.

But the first boy was very much embarrassed, offended, and he could not find how to answer him. Frustrated, angry, and also feeling guilty because, "My master said not to talk with these people. These people really are dangerous. Now, what kind of answer is this? He has humiliated me."

He went to his master and told him what had happened. "I am sorry that I talked to him. You were right, those people are strange. What kind of answer is this? I asked him, 'Where are you going?'—a simple formal question—and I knew he was going to the market, just as I was going to the market. But he said, 'Wherever the winds take me.'"

The master said, "I warned you, but you didn't listen. Now look, tomorrow you stand at the same place again. When he comes ask him, 'Where are you going?' and he will say, 'Wherever the winds take me.' Then you also be a little more philosophical. Say, 'If you don't have any legs, then? Because the soul is bodiless and the wind cannot take the soul anywhere!' What about that?"

Absolutely ready, the whole night the boy repeated it again and again and again. And next morning, very early, he went there, stood on the right spot, and at the exact time the second boy came again. The first boy was very happy, now he was going to show him what real philosophy is. So he asked, "Where are you going?" And he was waiting . . .

But the second boy said, "I am going to fetch vegetables from the market."

* * *

Now, what to do with the philosophy that he had learned?

Life is like that. You cannot prepare for it, you cannot be ready for it. That is its beauty, that is its wonder, that it always takes you unawares, it always comes as a surprise. If you have eyes you will see that each moment is a surprise and no ready-made answer is ever applicable.

I simply teach you an intrinsic law of life. Be obedient to your own self, be a light unto yourself and follow the light, and this problem will never arise. Then whatever you do is the thing to do, and whatever you don't do is the thing that has not to be done . . .

And the only way to be in contact with life, the only way not to lag behind life, is to have a heart that is not guilty, a heart that is innocent. Forget all about what you have been told—what has to be done and what has not to be done—nobody else can decide that for you.

Avoid those pretenders who want to decide for you; take the reins in your own hands. You have to decide. In fact, in that very decisiveness, your soul is born. When others decide for you, your soul remains asleep and dull. When you start deciding on your own, a sharpness arises. To decide means to take risks, to decide means you may be doing wrong—who knows, that is the risk. Who knows what is going to happen? That is the risk; there is no guarantee.

With the old, there is a guarantee. Millions and millions of people have followed it. How can so many people be wrong? That is the guarantee. If so many people say it is right, it must be right.

Take all the risks that are needed to be an individual, and accept the challenges so that they can sharpen you, can give you brilliance and intelligence.

Truth is not a belief, it is utter intelligence. It is a flaring-up of the hidden sources of your life; it is an enlightening experience of your consciousness. But you will have to provide the right space for it to happen. And the right space is accepting your-self as you are. Don't deny anything, don't become split, don't feel guilty.

UNCLING TO MISERY

It should be easy to drop suffering, anguish, misery. It should not be difficult: you don't want to be miserable, so there must be some deep complication behind it. The complication is that from your very childhood you have not been allowed to be happy, to be blissful, to be joyous.

You have been forced to be serious, and seriousness implies sadness. You were forced to do things that you never wanted to do. You were helpless, weak, dependent on people; naturally you had to do what they were saying. You did those things unwill-ingly, miserably, in deep resistance. Against yourself, you have been forced to do so much that by and by one thing became clear to you: that anything that is against you is right, and any-thing that is not against you is bound to be wrong. And con-stantly, this whole upbringing filled you with sadness, which is not natural.

To be joyous is natural, just as to be healthy is natural. When you are healthy, you don't go to the doctor to inquire, "Why am I healthy?" There is no need for any question about your health. But when you are sick, you immediately ask, "Why am I sick? What is the reason, the cause of my disease?"

It is perfectly right to ask why you are miserable. It is not right to ask why you are blissful. You have been brought up in an insane society where to be blissful without reason is thought to be madness. If you are simply smiling for no reason at all, people will think something is loose in your head—why are you smiling?

why are you looking so happy? And if you say, "I don't know, I am just being happy," your answer will only strengthen their idea that something has gone wrong with you.

But if you are miserable, nobody will ask why you are miserable. To be miserable is natural; everybody is. It is nothing special to you. You are not doing something unique.

Unconsciously this idea goes on settling in you, that misery is natural and blissfulness is unnatural. Blissfulness has to be proved. Misery needs no proof. Slowly it sinks deeper into you—into your blood, into your bones, into your marrow—although naturally it is against you. So you have been forced to be schizophrenic; something that is against your nature has been forced on you. You have been distracted from yourself into something which you are not.

This creates the whole misery of humanity, that everyone is where he should not be, what he should not be. And because man cannot be where he needs to be—where it is his birthright to be—he is miserable. You have been in this state of going farther and farther away from yourself; you have forgotten the way back home. So wherever you are, you think this is your home—misery has become your home, anguish has become your nature. Suffering has been accepted as health, not as sickness.

And when somebody says, "Drop this miserable life, drop this suffering that you are carrying unnecessarily," a very significant question arises: "This is all that I have! If I drop it I will be no one, I will lose my identity. At least right now I am somebody—somebody miserable, somebody sad, somebody in suffering. If I drop all this then the question will be, what is my identity? Who am I? I don't know the way back home, and you have taken away the hypocrisy, the false home that was created by the society."

Nobody wants to stand naked in the street.

It is better to be miserable—at least you have something to wear, although it is misery—but there is no harm; everyone else is wearing the same kind of clothes. For those who can afford it, their miseries are costly. Those who cannot afford it are doubly miserable—they have to live in a poor kind of misery, nothing much to brag about.

So there are rich miserable people and poor miserable people. And the poor miserable people are trying their hardest to somehow reach the status of rich miserable people. These are the only two types available.

The third type has been completely forgotten. The third is your reality, and it has no misery in it. Man's intrinsic nature is blissful.

Blissfulness is not something to be achieved.

It is already there; we are born with it.

We have not lost it, we have simply gone farther away, keeping our backs to ourselves.

It is just behind us; a small turn and a great revolution.

But there are fake religions all over the world which are telling you that you are miserable because in the past life you committed evil acts. All nonsense. Because why should existence wait for one life to punish you? There seems to be no need. In nature things happen immediately. You put your hand in the fire in this life and in the next life you will be burned? Strange! You will be burned immediately, here and now. Cause and effect are connected; there cannot be any distance.

But these fake religions go on consoling people: "Don't be worried. Just do good acts, worship more. Go to temple or church, and in the next life you will not be miserable." Nothing seems to be cash; everything is in the next life. And nobody comes back from the next life and says, "These people are telling absolute lies."

Religion is cash, it is not even a check.

Different religions have found different strategies, but the reason behind them is the same. Christians, Jews, Mohammedans, religions born outside India say to people, "You are suffering because Adam and Eve committed a sin." The first couple, thousands of years back . . . and not a great sin—you are committing it every day. They simply ate apples, and God had forbidden them to eat apples.

The problem is not apples, the problem is that they disobeyed. Thousands of years back somebody disobeyed God. And he was punished, he was thrown out of the Garden of Eden, thrown out of God's paradise. Why are we suffering?—because they were our forefathers.

Reality is something totally different. It is not a question of evil acts, it is a question of your having been taken away from yourself, from your natural blissfulness. And no religion wants you to be so easily blissful; otherwise what will happen to their disciplines? What will happen to their great practices, ascetic practices?

If dropping the misery is as easy as I say it is, then all these fake religions lose their business. It is a question of their business. Blissfulness has to be made so difficult—almost impossible—that people can only hope for it in some future life, after long arduous journeys.

But I say to you on my authority: it has happened to me so easily. I have also lived many past lives and certainly I must have committed more evil acts than any of you—because I don't consider them to be evil acts. Appreciation of beauty, appreciation of taste, appreciation of everything that makes life more livable, more lovable, are not evil things to me.

I want you to become sensitive, aesthetically sensitive to all these things. They will make you more human, they will create more softness in you, more gratitude toward existence.

And it is not a theoretical question with me. I have just accepted nothingness as a door—which I call meditation, which is nothing but another name for nothingness. And the moment nothingness happens, suddenly you are standing face to face with yourself, and all misery disappears.

The first thing you do is simply to laugh at yourself, at what an idiot you have been. That misery was never there; you were creating it with one hand and you were trying to destroy it with the other hand—and naturally you were split, in a schizophrenic condition.

It is absolutely easy, simple.

The most simple thing in existence is to be yourself.

It needs no effort; you are already there.

Just a remembrance . . . just getting out of all those stupid ideas that society has imposed on you. And that is as simple as a snake slipping out of its old skin and never even looking back. It is just an old skin, nothing more.

If you understand it, it can happen at this very moment.

Because at this very moment you can see there is no misery, no anguish.

You are silent, standing on the door of nothing; just a step more inward and you have found the greatest treasure that has been waiting for you for thousands of lives.

BE CONSCIOUS OF BLISS

Ordinarily the mind is always conscious of pain, never conscious of bliss. If you have a headache you are conscious of it. When you don't have a headache you are not conscious of the well-being of the head. When the body hurts you are conscious of it, but when the body is perfectly healthy you are not conscious of the health.

This is the root cause of why we feel so miserable: our whole consciousness is focused on pain. We only count the thorns—we never look at the flowers. Somehow we select the thorns and neglect the flowers. If we are wounded and continuously hurt, there is no surprise in it; it has to be so. For a certain biological reason it has happened: nature makes you aware of pain so that you can avoid it. It is a built-in system. Otherwise, your hand may be burning and you may not be conscious of it, and it will be difficult to survive. So nature has made it essential and inevitable that you have to be conscious of the pain. But nature has no built-in mechanism to make you conscious of pleasure, joy, bliss. That has to be learned, that has to be worked out. That is an art.

From this moment start becoming aware of things that are not natural. For example, your body is feeling perfectly healthy: sit silently, become conscious of it. Enjoy the well-being. Nothing is wrong—enjoy it! Make a deliberate effort to be conscious of it. You have eaten well and your body is satisfied, contented; become conscious of it.

When you are hungry, nature makes you conscious, but nature has no system to make you conscious of when you are satiated; that has to be grown. Nature need not grow it because survival is all that nature wants; more than that is luxury. Bliss is luxury, the greatest luxury.

And this is my observation about why people are so miserable—they are not really as miserable as they look. They have many moments of great joy, but those moments pass by; they never become aware of them. Their memories remain full of pain and wounds. Their minds remain full of nightmares. Not that there are not beautiful dreams and poetic visions—they are also there, but nobody is there to take note of them. In twenty-four hours' time thousands of things happen for which you would feel grateful to God, but you don't take note!

That has to be started from this moment. And you will be surprised that bliss will grow more and more every day, and, proportionately, pain and misery will become less and less. And the moment comes when life is almost a celebration. Pain is only once in a while, and that pain is part of the game. One is not distracted by it, not disturbed by it. One accepts it.

If you enjoy the satiation that comes after you have eaten, naturally you know that when you are hungry there will be a little pain . . . and that is good. When you have slept a good night's sleep and in the morning you are feeling so fresh and alive, rejuvenated, naturally if one night you cannot sleep, there will be a little agony, but that is part of the game also.

My own experience is that life consists of 99 percent bliss and one percent pain. But people's lives consist of 99 percent pain and one percent bliss; everything is upside-down.

Become more and more conscious of pleasure, joy, the positive, the flowers, the silver linings in the black dark clouds.

CHAPTER THREE

Basic Conditions for
Well-being

*L*isten to the body. *The body is not your enemy, and when the body is saying something, do accordingly, because the body has a wisdom of its own. Don't disturb it, don't go on a mind trip. I don't teach rigid rules, I simply give you a sense of awareness. Listen to your body.*

The body is your friend; it is not your enemy. Listen to its language, decode its language, and by and by, as you enter into the book of the body and you turn its pages, you will become aware of the whole mystery of life. Condensed it is, in your body. Magnified a millionfold, it is all over the world. But condensed in a small formula, it is there, present, in your body.

MAKE CONTACT WITH THE BODY

You are not in contact with many things in your body, you are just carrying your body. Contact means a deep sensitivity. You may not even feel your body. It happens that only when you are ill do you feel your body. There is a headache, then you feel the head; without the headache there is no contact with the head. When there is pain in the leg, you become aware of the leg. You become aware only when something goes wrong.

If everything is okay you remain completely unaware, and, really, that is the moment when contact can be made—when everything is okay—because when something goes wrong then that contact is made with illness, with something that has gone wrong and the well-being is no more there. You have the head right now, then a headache comes and you make contact. The contact is made not with the head but with the headache. With the head contact is possible only when there is no headache and the head is filled with well-being, but we have almost lost the capacity. We don't have any contact when we are okay. So our contact is just an emergency measure. There is a headache: some repair is needed, some medicine is needed, something has to be done, so you make the contact and do something.

Try to make contact with your body when everything is good. Just lie down on the grass, close your eyes, and feel the sensation that is going on within, the well-being that is bubbling. Lie down in a river. The water is touching the body and every cell is being cooled. Feel inside how that coolness enters cell by cell, goes deep into the body. The body is a great phenomenon, one of the miracles of nature.

Sit in the sun. Let the sunrays penetrate the body. Feel the warmth as it moves within, as it goes deeper, as it touches your blood cells and reaches to the very bones. And sun is life, the very source, so with closed eyes just feel what is happening. Remain alert, watch and enjoy. By and by you will become aware of a very subtle harmony, a very beautiful music continuously going on inside. Then you have contact with the body; otherwise you carry a dead body.

It is just like this: a person who loves his car has a different type of contact and relationship with the car than a person who doesn't. A person who doesn't love his car goes on driving it and he treats it as a mechanism, but a person who loves his car will become aware of even the smallest change in the mood of the car, the slightest change of sound. Something is changing in the car and suddenly he will become aware of it. No one else has heard it. The passengers are sitting there; they have not heard it. But a slight change in the sound of the engine, any clicking, any change, and the person who loves his car will become aware of it. He has a deep contact. He is not only driving, the car is not just a mechanism; rather he has spread himself into the car and he has allowed the car to enter him.

Your body can be used as a mechanism, then you need not be very sensitive about it. And the body goes on saying many things you never hear because you don't have any contact with it.

In Russia new research went on for some decades, and their scientists have concluded many things. One very revealing result is this: whenever a disease happens, for six months continuously before it happens the body gives signals to you. And six months is such a long time! If a disease is going to happen next year, in the middle of this year the body will start giving you signals—but you don't receive the signals, you don't understand, you don't know. When the disease manifests itself, only then will you become aware. Or even then you may not be aware—your doctor first becomes aware that you have some deep trouble inside.

One person who was conducting this research for many years made films and cameras that can detect a disease before it actually happens. He says that the disease can be treated, and the patient will never become aware of whether it existed or not. If a cancer is going to happen next year, it can be treated right now. There are no physical indications, but just in the body electricity things are changing—not in the body, but in the body electricity, in the bioenergy, things are changing. First they will change in the bioenergy and then they will descend to the physical.

If they can be treated in the bioenergy layer, then they will never come to the physical body. Because of this research it may become possible in the coming century that no one need be ill, that there will be no more need to go to the hospital. Before the disease actually comes to the body it can be treated, but it has to be detected by a mechanical device. You cannot detect it, and you are living there in your body. There is no contact. You may have heard many stories that Hindu sannyasins, rishis, Zen monks, Buddhist bhikkus, declare their death before it happens. And you may be surprised to know that that declaration is always made six months before it happens—never more, always six months before. Many saints have declared that they are going to die, but just six months before. It is not accidental; those six months are meaningful. Before the physical body dies the bioenergy starts dying, and a person who is in deep contact with his bioenergy knows that now the energy has started shrinking. Life means spreading, death means shrinking. He feels that the life energy is shrinking; he declares that he will be dead within six months. Zen monks are known to have even chosen how to die—because they know.

It happened once:

One Zen monk was to die, so he asked his disciples, "Suggest to me how to die, in what posture."

That man was a little eccentric, a little crazy, a mad old man but very beautiful.

His disciples started laughing; they thought that he may have been joking because he was always joking. So somebody suggested, "How about dying standing in the corner of the temple?"

The man said, "But I have heard a story that in the past one monk has died standing, so that won't be good. Suggest something unique."

So somebody said, "Die while just walking in the garden."

He said, "I have heard that somebody in China once died walking."

Then someone suggested a really unique idea: "Stand in *shirshasana,* the headstand, and die." Nobody has ever died standing on his head, it is very difficult to die standing on the head. Even to sleep standing on the head is impossible, death is too difficult. Even to sleep is impossible and death is a great sleep. It is impossible—even ordinary sleep is impossible.

The man accepted the idea. He enjoyed it. He said, "This is good."

They thought that he was just joking, but he stood in headstand. They became afraid: What is he doing? And what to do now? And they thought he was almost dead. It was weird—a dead person standing in headstand. They became scared, so somebody suggested, "He has a sister in the nearby monastery who is a great nun. Go and fetch her. She is the elder sister of this man and may do something with him. She knows him well."

The sister came. It is said that she came and said, "Ikkyu"—Ikkyu was the name of the monk—"don't be foolish! This is no way to die."

Ikkyu laughed, jumped down from his headstand, and said, "Okay, so what is the right way?"

She said, "Sit in *padmasana,* in the Buddha posture, and die. This is no way to die. You have always been a foolish man—everybody will laugh."

So it is said he sat in the Buddha posture and died, and then the sister left—a beautiful man. But how could he decide that he was going to die? And even to choose the posture! The bioenergy started shrinking, he could feel it—but this feeling comes only when you have a deep contact not only with the surface of the body but with the roots.

So first try to be more and more sensitive about your body. Listen to it; it goes on saying many things, and you are so head-oriented you never listen to it. Whenever there is a conflict between your mind and body, your body is almost always going to be right more than your mind, because the body is natural, your mind is societal; the body belongs to this vast nature, and your mind belongs to your society, your particular society, age, time. Body has deep roots in existence, mind is just wavering on the surface. But you always listen to the mind, you never listen to the body. Because of this long habit contact is lost.

You have the heart, and heart is the root, but you don't have any contact with it. First start having contact with the body. Soon you will become aware that the whole body vibrates around the center of the heart just as the whole solar system moves around the sun. Hindus have called the heart the sun of the body. The whole body is a solar system and moves around the heart. You became alive when the heart started beating, you will die when the heart stops beating. The heart remains the solar center of your body. Become alert to it. But you can become alert, by and by, only if you become alert to the whole body.

BE TRUE TO YOURSELF

Remember to be true to yourself. How? Three things have to be remembered. One, never listen to anybody, what they say for you to be: always listen to your inner voice, what you would like to be. Otherwise your whole life will be wasted.

Thousand and one are the temptations around you because

many people are there peddling their wares. It is a supermarket, the world, and everybody is interested in selling his wares to you; everybody is a salesman. If you listen to too many salesmen you will become mad. Don't listen to anybody, just close your eyes and listen to the inner voice. That is what meditation is all about: to listen to the inner voice. This is the first thing.

Then the second thing—if you have done the first thing only then the second becomes possible: never wear a mask. If you are angry, be angry. It is risky, but don't smile, because that is to be untrue. But you have been taught that when you are angry, smile; then your smile becomes false, a mask . . . just an exercise of the lips, nothing else. The heart full of anger, poison, and the lips smiling—you become a false phenomenon.

Then the other thing also happens: when you want to smile you cannot smile. Your whole mechanism is topsy-turvy because when you wanted to be angry you weren't, when you wanted to hate you didn't. Now you want to love; suddenly you find that the mechanism doesn't function. Now you want to smile; you have to force it. Really your heart is full of smile and you want to laugh loudly, but you cannot laugh, something chokes in the heart, something chokes in the throat. The smile doesn't come, or even if it comes it is a very pale and dead smile. It doesn't make you happy. You don't bubble up with it. There is not a radiance around you.

When you want to be angry, be angry. There is nothing wrong in being angry. If you want to laugh, laugh. There is nothing wrong in laughing loudly. By and by you will see that your whole system is functioning. When it functions, really, it has a hum around it, just as a car, when everything is going good, hums. The driver who loves his car knows that now everything is functioning well, there is an organic unity—the mechanism is functioning well. You can see: whenever a person's mechanism is functioning well, you can hear the hum around him. He walks, but his step has a dance in it. He talks, but his words carry a subtle poetry in them. He looks at you, and he really looks; his glance is not just lukewarm, it is really warm. When he touches you he really touches you; you can feel his energy moving into your body, a current of life being transferred . . . because his mechanism is functioning well.

Don't wear masks; otherwise you will create dysfunctions in your mechanism—blocks. There are many blocks in your body. A person who has been suppressing anger, his jaw becomes blocked. All the anger comes up to the jaw and then stops there. His hands become ugly. They don't have the graceful movement of a dancer; that is because the anger flows into the fingers—and they become blocked. Remember, anger has two sources to be released from. One is teeth, another is fingers. All animals, when they are angry, will bite you with their teeth or they will start tearing at you with their hands. Therefore the nails and the teeth are the two points from which the anger is released.

I have a suspicion that whenever anger is suppressed for too long, people develop tooth trouble. Their teeth go wrong because too much energy is there and is never released. And anybody who suppresses anger will eat more; angry people will always eat more because their teeth need some exercise. Angry people will smoke more. Angry people will talk more; they can become obsessive talkers because, somehow, the jaw needs exercise so that the energy will be released a little bit. And angry people's hands will become knotted, ugly. If the energy was released they could have beautiful hands.

If you suppress anything, in the body there is some part, a corresponding part, to the emotion. If you don't want to cry, your eyes will lose their luster because tears are needed. When once in a while you weep and cry and really get into it—when you become it and the tears start flowing down your eyes—your eyes are cleansed, and they again become fresh, young, and virgin. That's why women have more beautiful eyes, because they can still cry. Men no longer have vibrant eyes because they have a wrong notion that men should not cry. If somebody, a small boy cries, even the parents as well as others say, "What are you doing? Are you being a sissy?"

What nonsense, because nature has given you—man, woman—the same tear glands. If man was not to weep, he would have no tear glands. Simple mathematics. Why do the tear glands exist in man in the same proportion as they exist in woman? Eyes need weeping and crying, and it is really beautiful if you can cry and weep wholeheartedly.

Remember, if you cannot cry and weep wholeheartedly, you also cannot laugh because that is the other polarity. People who can laugh can also cry; people who cannot cry cannot laugh. And you may have observed sometimes in children that if they laugh loudly and long they start crying—because both things are joined. I have heard mothers saying to their children, "Don't laugh too much; otherwise you will start crying." That is really true, because the phenomena are not different—just the same energy moves to the opposite poles.

The second thing is, don't use masks—be true whatever the cost.

And the third thing to remember is authenticity: always remain in the present, because all falseness enters either from the past or from the future. That which has passed has passed—don't bother about it. And don't carry it as a burden; otherwise it will not allow you to be authentic to the present. And all that has not come has not come yet—don't bother unnecessarily about the future; otherwise the future will come into the present and destroy it. Be true to the present, and then you will be authentic. To be in the here and now is to be authentic.

RELAX INTO LIFE AS IT COMES

Society certainly prepares you for activity, for ambition, for speed, for efficiency. It does not prepare you to relax and do nothing and to rest. It condemns all kinds of restfulness as laziness. It condemns people who are not madly active—because the whole society is madly active, always trying to reach somewhere. Nobody knows exactly where, but everybody is concerned: "Go faster!"

I have heard about a man and his wife driving on a road as fast as they can. The wife was telling the man again and again, "Just look at the map."

And the man was saying, "You keep quiet. Shut up! I am the driver. It doesn't matter where we are going, what matters is that we are going with speed. The real thing is speed." Nobody in the world knows where they are going, and why they are going there.

There is a very famous anecdote about George Bernard Shaw. He was traveling from London to some other place and the ticket collector came. He looked in all his pockets, in his bag, then he opened his suitcase. And the ticket collector said, "I know you. Everybody knows you. You are George Bernard Shaw. You are a world-famous man. The ticket must be there, you must have forgotten where you have put it. Don't be worried. Leave it."

George Bernard Shaw said to the man, "You don't understand my problem. I'm not looking for the ticket just to show you. I want to know where I am going. That stupid ticket—if it is lost, I am lost. You think I am looking for the ticket for you? You tell me where I am going."

The ticket collector said, "That is too much. I was just trying to help you. Don't get disturbed. Maybe you can remember it later on by the time you reach the station. How can I tell you where you are going?"

But everybody is in the same position. It is good that there are no spiritual ticket collectors around, checking, "Where are you going?" Otherwise you would be simply standing around without any answer. You have been going somewhere; there is no doubt about it. Your whole life you have been going somewhere, but you don't actually know where you are going.

You eventually reach a graveyard, that is one thing that's certain. But that is the one place you were not going to, the one place nobody wants to go to, but everyone finally gets there. That is the terminus where all trains end up. If you don't have a ticket, wait for the terminus. And then they say, "Get down. The train goes no farther."

The whole society is geared for work. It is a workaholic society. It does not want you to learn relaxation, so from the very childhood it plants antirelaxation ideas in your mind.

I am not telling you to relax for the whole day. Do your work, but find out some time for yourself, and that can be found only in relaxation. And you will be surprised that if you can relax for an hour or two hours out of each twenty-four hours, it will give you a deeper insight into yourself.

It will change your behavior outwardly—you will become more calm, more quiet. It will change the quality of your work— it will be more artistic and more graceful. You will be committing fewer mistakes than you used to, because now you are more together, more centered.

Relaxation has miraculous powers. It is not laziness. From the outside, the lazy man may look as if he is not working at anything, but his mind is going as fast as it can. The relaxed man—his body is relaxed, his mind is relaxed, his heart is relaxed—for two hours he is almost absent. In these two hours his body recovers, his heart recovers, his intelligence recovers, and you will see that in his work.

He will not be a loser—although he will not be frantic anymore, he will not be unnecessarily running hither and thither. He will go directly to the point where he wants to go. And he will do things that are needed to be done; he will not be doing anything unnecessary. He will say only that which is needed to be said. His words will become telegraphic; his movements will become graceful; his life will become poetry.

Relaxation can transform you and transport you to such beautiful heights—and the technique is so simple. There is nothing much to it. For a few days you will find it difficult because of old habits. To break down the old habits takes a few days.

With deeper and deeper relaxation it becomes meditation. Meditation is the name of the deepest relaxation.

ALLOW THE WISDOM OF THE BODY

The body has great wisdom—allow it. Allow it more and more to follow its own wisdom. And whenever you have time, just relax. Let your breathing go on on its own. Do not interfere. Our habit to interfere has become so ingrained that you cannot even breathe without interference. If you watch your breathing, you will immediately see you have started to interfere. You begin taking deep breaths, or you start exhaling more. There is no need to interfere at all. Just let your breath be as it is; your body knows exactly what it needs. If it needs more oxygen it will breathe more; if it needs less oxygen it will breathe less.

Just leave it all to your body! Become absolutely noninter-fering. And wherever you feel any tension anywhere, relax that part. And slowly, slowly . . . First begin while you are sitting, resting, and then while you are doing things. When you are cleaning the floor or working in the kitchen or in the office, keep that relaxedness. Action need not be an interference in your re-laxed state. And then there is a beauty, a great beauty, to your ac-tivity. Your activity will have the flavor of meditativeness.

But people go on making unnecessary efforts. Sometimes their efforts are their barriers; their efforts are the problems that they are creating.

> There was a lot of confusion downtown during the big snowstorm. Mulla Nasruddin went over to help a fat lady get into a taxi cab. After rushing and shoving and slipping on the ice, he told her he did not think he could get her in.
> She said, "In? I am trying to get out!"

Just observe . . . There are things where if you push, you will miss. Don't push the river at all, and don't try to go upstream. The river is flowing toward the ocean of its own accord—just be part of it, be part of its journey. It will take you to the ultimate.

If we relax, we will know; if we don't relax, we will not know. Relaxation becomes the door to that great knowing—enlightenment.

A SYMPHONY OF JOY

Really, joy only means that your body is in a symphony, nothing else—that your body is in a musical rhythm, nothing else. Joy is not pleasure; pleasure has to be derived from something else. Joy is just being yourself—alive, fully vibrant, vital. A feeling of a subtle music around your body and within your body, a symphony—that is joy. You can be joyful when your body is flowing, when it is a riverlike flow.

The healthy organism is always capable of achieving peaks of orgasm. It is orgasmic. It is streaming, flowing.

When a happy man laughs, he laughs as if his whole body laughs. It is not just the lips, it is not just the face. From the feet to the head he laughs as a total organism. Ripples of laughter flow through his being. His whole bioenergy is rippled through with laughter. It is in a dance. When a healthy man is sad, he's really sad, totally. When a healthy man is angry, he is really angry, totally. When he makes love, he is love; nothing else. When he makes love, he only makes love.

In fact, to say that he makes love is not right. The expression in English is vulgar because love cannot be made. It is not that he makes love—he is love. He is nothing but love energy. And that's the way he is in all that he does. If he is walking, he is just a walking energy. There is no walker in it. If he is digging a hole, he is just the digging.

A healthy man is not an entity; he is a process, a dynamic process. Or we can say that a healthy man is not a noun but a verb—not a river but a rivering. He is continuously flowing in all dimensions, overflowing. And any society that prevents this is pathological. Any person who is inhibited in any way is pathological, lopsided. Only a part, not the whole, is functioning.

Many women don't know what orgasm is. Many men don't know what a total orgasm is. Many achieve only a local orgasm, a genital orgasm; it is confined to the genitals. Just a small ripple in the genitals—and finished. It is not like possession when the whole body moves into a whirlpool and you are lost in an abyss.

For a few moments time stops and the mind does not function. For a few moments you do not know who you are. That is a total orgasm.

Man is unhealthy and pathological because society has crippled him in many ways. You are not allowed to love totally, you are not allowed to be angry; you are not allowed to be yourself. A thousand and one limitations are enforced.

If you really want to be healthy, you have to uninhibit yourself. You have to undo all that society has done to you. Society is very criminal, but that is the only society we have, so nothing can be done right now. Each person has to work his own way out of this pathological society, and the best way is to start becoming orgasmic in as many ways as possible.

If you go swimming, then swim, but swim as a total being so you become swimming, a verb; the noun is dissolved. If you run, then run; then becoming running, not a runner. In your Olympics you have runners, egos, competitors . . . all ambitious. If you can simply run without the runner being there, that running becomes Zen; it becomes meditative. Dance, but don't become a dancer, because the dancer starts manipulating and then he is not total. Just dance and let the dance take you wherever it wants to.

Allow life, trust life, and by and by life will destroy all your inhibitions, and energy will start streaming in all those parts where it has been prevented.

So whatever you do, do it with this hidden idea that you have to become more flowing. If you hold somebody's hand, really hold it. You are holding it anyway, so why waste this moment? Really hold it! Don't just be two dead hands holding each other, each wondering when the other is going to leave. If you talk, then let the talk be passionate; otherwise you will bore others and yourself.

Life should be a passion, a vibrating passion, a pulsating passion, a tremendous energy. Whatever you do should not be dull; otherwise don't do it. There is no duty to do anything, but whatever you feel like doing, really do it.

All inhibitions will disappear by and by, and your whole life will be reclaimed. Your body will be reclaimed; your mind will be reclaimed. Society has crippled the body, the mind—everything. It has given you certain choices; very narrow slits are open and you can only see through those slits. You are not allowed to see the total.

LAUGH AND BE WHOLE

Humor will join your split parts, humor will glue your fragments into one whole. Have you not observed it? When you laugh a hearty laugh, suddenly all fragments disappear and you become one. When you laugh, your soul and your body are one—they laugh together. When you think, your body and soul are separate. When you cry, your body and soul are one; they function in harmony.

Remember always that all those things are good, for the good, which make you one whole. Laughter, crying, dancing, singing—all those makes you one piece, in which you function as one harmony, not separate. Thinking can go on in the head, and the body can go on doing a thousand and one things; you can continue eating, and the mind can continue thinking. This is split. You walk along the road: the body is walking and you are thinking; not thinking of the road, not thinking of the trees that surround it, not thinking of the sun, not thinking of the people who are passing, but thinking of other things, of other worlds.

But laugh, and if the laugh is really deep, if it is not a

pseudo-laugh, just on the lips, suddenly you feel your body and your soul are functioning together. It is not only in the body, it goes deepest into your core. It arises from your very being and spreads toward the circumference. You are one in laughter.

In a New England resort town there was a man so homely that he was the butt of every practical joke that the townsfolk could think up. A plastic surgeon who visited the resort on a vacation was so touched by his ugliness that he offered to change the man's face without charge. "In fact," he said, "just for the heck of it, I will do some plastic surgery that will make you the handsomest man in New England."

Just before he put the man under the knife, the surgeon said, "Do you want me to change your face completely, totally?"

"No," answered the man, "not too much. I want the fellows to know who it is who is so handsome."

This is how the ego functions. You want the fellows to know who it is who is so handsome. You want the fellows to know who it is who is so meek, so humble, who it is who is standing at the back of the queue. If even that much desire is there the ego is completely alive, thriving. Nothing has changed. Only a total change is a change.

Sammy Goldberg loses a lot of money on the stock market and is in a terrible state. He goes to visit his doctor and says, "Doctor, doctor, my hands won't stop shaking."

"Tell me," says the doctor, "do you drink a lot?"

"I can't," says Sammy, "I spill most of it."

"I see," says the doctor and then proceeds to give Sammy

a thorough examination. When he has finished, he says, "Tell me, do you get a tingling in your arms, aches in your knees, and sudden dizzy spells?"

"Yes," replies Sammy, "that's exactly what I get."

"That's funny," says the doctor, "so do I . . . I wonder what it is!"

Then the doctor refers to his notes for several minutes before looking up and saying, "Tell me, have you had this before?"

"Yes," says Sammy, "I have."

"Well, there you are, then," replies the doctor, pressing the buzzer for the next patient. "You have got it again!"

When Fred comes back from visiting the doctor, he looks terrible. He tells his wife, Becky, that the doctor had said that he was going to die before the night was out. She hugs him, and they cry a little, and Becky suggests they go to bed early to make love one more time.

They make love until Becky falls asleep, but Fred is afraid to sleep because it is his last night on earth. He lies there in the dark while Becky snores.

Fred whispers in his wife's ear, "Becky, please, just one more time for old times' sake." But Becky keeps on snoring.

Fred looks at his watch, leans over to his wife, and shakes her hard. "Please, Becky, just one more time for old times' sake!"

Becky simply looks at him and says, "Fred, how can you be so selfish? It is all right for you, but I have to get up in the morning."

All old people are doing that everywhere in every family, just testing the peace of their relatives.

Sammy Goldberg looked very sad; his wife was sick, so he called the doctor. After examining Mrs. Goldberg, the doctor said to Sammy, "I am afraid it is bad news: your wife has only a few hours to live. I hope you understand there is nothing more to be done. Don't let yourself suffer."

"It is all right, doc," said Goldberg, "I have suffered for forty years, I can suffer a few more hours."

Just remember the definition of health. When you don't feel your body at all, your body is healthy. You feel your head only when you have a headache. When you don't have any headache, you don't have any head either—it is simply light, it has no weight. When your legs are hurting, you have them. When they are not hurting, they are absent. When the body is healthy—my definition of health is that you are absolutely unaware of its existence, whether it is there or not makes no difference.

And the same is true about the healthy mind. It is only the insane mind that is felt. When the mind is sane, silent, it is not felt. When the body and mind both are in stillness, your soul can be experienced more easily, with laughter. There is no need to be serious at all.

Sammy Goldberg went to his doctor, feeling very run down due to worry over money matters. "Relax," the doctor ordered, "just two weeks ago I had another fellow who was upset because he could not pay his tailor's bills. I told him to forget them and now he feels great."

"I know," said Goldberg, "I am his tailor."

Now, there are situations . . . But if you are a little alert, even in the situation of Sammy Goldberg, you would have laughed. You will find such ridiculous situations everywhere. Life is full of them.

A man got on the bus with at least a dozen children. A little old lady asked him if they were all his.

"Of course not," the man snapped. "I am a contraceptive salesman and these are all complaints."

Just look around, you will find many such situations. Learn the art of enjoying them.

Joe had been bitten by a dog. The wound was taking a long time to heal, so he went to see his doctor, who ordered that the dog to be brought in. Just as the doctor suspected, the dog had rabies. "I am afraid it is too late to give you serum," the doctor told Joe.

Joe sat down at the doctor's desk and begin to write fanatically. "Perhaps it won't be so bad," consoled the doctor, "there is no need to write your will right now."

"I am not making out my will," replied Joe, "I am just writing out a list of people I am going to bite."

If nothing can be done and I am going to be mad, then why not use the opportunity? Such a great opportunity . . .

Enjoy life, laugh at the ridiculousness of things all around. Laugh the whole way to God's temple. Those who have laughed enough have reached it; the serious people are still wandering around with long faces.

Young Dr. Dagburt goes out with Dr. Bones, a general practitioner, to observe him on home visits. "I will conduct the first two," says Bones. "Watch closely, then you give it a try."

At the first house, they are met by a distressed man. "My wife is having terrible stomach cramps," he says.

Dr. Bones does a brief examination, then gets on his hands and knees and looks under the bed. "Madam," says Bones, "you must cut out your ridiculous intake of sweets and chocolate, and you will be well in a day." Dagburt peeks under the bed and sees candy wrappers littering the floor.

On the next call they are met by a distraught Becky Goldberg. "It is Sammy, doctor!" she cries. "He was very forgetful all day yesterday, and today he has been falling over a lot. When I put him to bed, he passed out."

Examining Sammy, Bones gets down on the floor and looks under the bed. "It is a very simple problem," Bones says to Sammy. "You are drinking too much!" Young Dr. Dagburt sneaks a look under the bed and sees seven empty gin bottles.

At the third house, it is Dagburt's turn. He rings the doorbell and there is a long delay before a flushed young woman answers.

"Your husband asked us to call," says Dagburt. "He said you were not yourself this morning, and asked us to give you an examination."

So they go upstairs, and the woman lies down. Dagburt examines her and then he looks under the bed. "Okay," he concludes, "I prescribe you follow a dairy-free diet and you will be fine."

As they are leaving, Bones is puzzled and asks, "How did you reach that conclusion about the dairy-free diet?"

"Well," says Dagburt, "I followed your example and looked under the bed—where I found a milkman!"

Slobovia meets Kowalski at the Pope and Hooker pub for a few midnight beers.

"How is your wife's cooking?" asks Kowalski.

"I came home tonight," says Slobovia, "and my wife was crying and weeping because the dog had eaten a pie she made for me. 'Don't cry,' I told her, 'I will buy you another dog.'"

"Mr. Klopman," says Dr. Bones, "even though you are a very sick man, I think I will be able to pull you through."

"Doctor," cries Klopman, "if you do that, when I get well, I will donate five thousand dollars to your new hospital."

Months later, Bones meets Klopman in the street. "How do you feel?" he asks.

"Wonderful, doctor, just fine!" says Klopman. "Never felt better!"

"I have been meaning to speak to you," says Bones. "What about the money for the new hospital?"

"What are you talking about?" asks Klopman.

"You said," replies Bones, "that if you got well, you would donate five thousand dollars for the new hospital."

"I said that?" asks Klopman. "That just shows how sick I was!"

Moishe Finkelstein's wife, Ruthie, is always complaining about his bad performance in bed, so Moishe goes to visit his doctor. Dr. Bones prescribes some new miracle pills that are sure to do the trick.

A month later, Moishe returns to see Dr. Bones. "The pills are fantastic," says Moishe. "I have been making love three times a night."

"That's great," chuckles Bones. "And what does your wife say about your lovemaking now?"

"Ah, I don't know," replies Moishe, "I have not been home yet."

* * *

It is a bright Monday morning in downtown Santa Banana, California. Getting ready for his first patients to arrive is the neospecialist in super-surgery, Dr. Decapitate. Dr. Decapitate looks around at his modern, high-tech, computerized, chromium-plated office, pushes a button, and in walks his first patient, Porky Poke.

"Doc!" cries Porky, his head wrapped in bandages.

"Ah! Don't tell me!" shouts Dr. Decapitate. "It is your head!"

"That is fantastic!" cries Porky. "How did you know?"

"I could tell immediately," replies Dr. Decapitate. "I have been in this business for thirty years!" Then the doctor fiddles with some switches and buttons on his computer, and cries, "There is no doubt about it—you have a splitting migraine headache."

"That is incredible!" says Porky. "I have had it all my life. Can you cure me?"

"Okay," says Decapitate, consulting his computer screen, "this may sound a little drastic, but there is only one way I can help. I will have to remove your left testicle."

"My God! My left ball?" cries Porky. "Well, okay. I will do anything to stop this headache!"

So one week later, Porky Poke waddles out of Decapitate's private surgery, missing his left nut, but feeling like a new man.

"It is gone!" cries Porky, trying to dance, but finding his movements painfully restricted. "My migraine is gone!"

To celebrate the occasion, Porky goes directly to Moishe Finkelstein's Tailoring Boutique to get a whole new wardrobe of clothes.

Moishe takes one look at Porky and says, "You must be a size forty-two jacket."

"That's right!" exclaims Porky. "How did you know?"

"I could tell immediately," replied Moishe, "I have been in this business for thirty years. And you wear a size thirty-six pants—with a thirty-four-inch inseam."

"Amazing!" shouts Porky. "That is incredible. You are absolutely right!"

"Of course I am right," replies Moishe. "I have been doing this all my life. And you take a size nine and a half shoe."

"Unbelievable!" cries Porky. "That is exactly right."

"And," says Moishe, "you wear a size four underwear."

"No!" replies Porky. "You are wrong. I wear a size three."

"That is not possible," snaps Moishe, taking a closer look. "You wear a size four underwear."

"Ah no, I don't!" says Porky. "All my life I have worn size three!"

"Okay," says Moishe, "you can wear a size three—but it is going to give you a terrible migraine!"

CHAPTER ∎ FOUR

Symptoms and
Solutions

*W*hen you are not behaving with your body naturally, some illness erupts. That illness is a friend. It shows: "Behave, change your ways! Somewhere you are going against nature." If you don't take food for three or four days, you feel dizzy, you feel hungry, you feel sad. The whole body is saying to you, "Take food!" because the body needs energy.

Always remember: Energy is neutral, so the whole quality of your being depends on you. You can be happy, you can be unhappy—it is up to you. Nobody else is responsible.

When you feel hungry, eat. When you feel thirsty, drink. When you feel sleepy, go to sleep. Don't force nature. For a little while you can force it, because that much freedom is there. If you want to fast, you can fast for a few days, but every day you will become weaker and weaker and weaker, and every day you will be in more and more misery. If you don't want to breathe, for a few seconds you can stop breathing, but only for a few seconds—that much freedom is possible. But that is not very much, and soon you will feel a choking, dying sensation if you don't breathe well.

All misery exists to indicate to you that somewhere you have gone wrong, you have gone off the track. Come back immediately! If you start listening to the body, listening to nature, listening to your inner being, you will be more and more happy. Become a good listener to nature.

[1] TENSION IN THE BELLY

Question: *"I often have a rocklike feeling in my stomach. How can I soften it up?"*

The majority of people suffer from a rocklike stomach. It is the cause of a thousand and one illnesses—physical, mental, both—because the stomach is the center where your psychology and your physiology meet; they meet at the navel. The navel is the contact point between psychology and physiology, so if the musculature becomes rocklike around the navel, you become very divided. Your mind and body become separate; then they are almost two things, with no bridge.

So sometimes you can do something that only the mind feels like doing but the body is not ready for. For example, you can eat: the body is not hungry but you can go on eating because the mind is enjoying the taste. It will not know how the body is feeling because the feeling is cut off; there is no bridge. Sometimes you can be so engaged in playing cards or seeing a movie that you may not know that your body is hungry. When this happens one remains like two parallel lines, never meeting. That's what schizophrenia is, and it is very rare to find a person who is not, in some way, schizophrenic. But one symptom is always present: a rocklike stomach.

So the first thing to do is to start exhaling deeply. And when you exhale deeply, naturally, you will have to pull the stomach in. Then relax and let the air rush in. If you have exhaled deeply, the air will rush in with such force. It will go like a hammering— it will destroy the rocklike structure around the stomach. This is the first step.

The second step: in the morning, after your bowel movement

when your stomach is empty, take a dry towel and rub your stomach, massage your stomach. Start from the right corner and go around, not the other way, and give a three-to-four-minute massage. That will also help to relax the stomach.

And the third step: whenever you can, do a little running. Running is very good—jogging, running. Do these three things, and within a month the rock will disappear.

[2] FEELING DISCONNECTED FROM THE BODY

Question: *"I don't feel my body. How can I get more in touch with it?"*

The first thing is to come back to the body. If we are not in contact with our bodies we are not in contact with the earth. We are uprooted, we don't have any roots, and without being rooted in the body, nothing can be done, nothing at all. Once you get rooted in the body everything becomes possible.

And problems like jealousy, possessiveness, and greed are all part of unrootedness. Because we are not rooted we are always afraid; because of that fear we become possessive, because of that fear we cannot trust anybody and so jealousy comes. In fact, we cannot trust ourselves—that is the problem—and how can you trust yourself when you don't have any roots in the earth? Trust comes when you have deep roots in the earth. Then, come whatever, you know that you will be able to stand it and face it. Then you don't cling to others—there is no need; you are enough alone.

So the first step is that you have to get more and more rooted in your body. Feel the body more, enjoy action, go running in the morning, and enjoy your body and the feel of running energy. Go swimming; enjoy your body and the river and the touch of water. Jog and dance and jump in the air and in the sun and let your body again start trembling with joy.

This has to be done first, and take as many deep breaths as possible. Once you get into your body, once you again become alive in your body, nine out of ten problems will disappear.

This is one of the tricks society has used to alienate people from themselves. It has cut your connection with body, so you are just like a ghost in a machine. You are in your body and not yet in your body—you are just hovering around. You take the hand of your friend in your hand but it is just a dead hand in a dead hand—there is no feeling, no poetry, no joy. You eat but you go on stuffing yourself; taste is lost. You see but you don't see the psychedelic existence as it is; you see dull colors, gray, dusty. You listen to music but just sound goes on falling; the music is missed.

So for a few months enjoy anything that is concerned with your body: running, jogging, playing, jumping, dancing, singing, shouting in the mountains. Bring back your childhood! And you will start feeling that you are being born again. You will have the feeling, exactly the same feeling as the caterpillar has when it becomes a butterfly.

[3] SHOULDER AND NECK PAIN

Question: *"I am a businessman and I get a bad pain in my shoulder when I'm in the marketplace. Doctors say it is psychosomatic and treat me with painkillers."*

A few things can be of very great help. One is Rolfing, or deep-tissue massage, and the second is acupuncture.

The pain will go—it is nothing to be worried about. Just remember a few things. One is that a Canadian psychoanalyst, Dr. Hans Selye, has been working his whole life on only one problem—that is stress. And he has come to certain profound conclusions. One is that stress is not always wrong; it can be used in beautiful ways. It is not necessarily negative, but if we think that it is negative, that it is not good, then we create problems. Stress in itself can be used as a stepping-stone; it can become a creative force. But ordinarily we have been taught down through the ages that stress is bad, that when you are in any kind of stress you become afraid. And your fear makes it even more stressful; the situation is not helped by it.

For example, there is something in the marketplace is creating the stress. The moment you feel this tension, this stress, you become afraid that this should not be so: "I have to relax." Now, trying to relax will not help, because you cannot relax; in fact, trying to relax will create a new kind of stress. The stress is there and you are trying to relax and you cannot, so you are complicating the problem.

When stress is there use it as creative energy. First, accept it; there is no need to fight with it. Accept it, it is perfectly okay. It simply says, "The market is not going well, something is going wrong," or "You may be a loser," or something else. Stress is simply an indication that the body is getting ready to fight. Now if you try to relax or you take painkillers or tranquilizers, you are going against the body. The body is getting ready to fight a certain situation, a certain challenge that is there: enjoy the challenge!

Even if sometimes you can't sleep at night there is no need to worry. Work it out, use that energy that is coming up: walk up and down, go for a run, go for a long walk, plan what you want to do, what the mind wants to do. Rather than trying to go to sleep, which is not possible, use the situation in a creative way. The energy simply says that the body is ready to fight with the problem; this is no time to relax. Relaxation can be done later on.

In fact, if you have lived your stress totally you will come to relaxation automatically; you can go on only so far, then the body automatically relaxes. If you want to relax in the middle you create trouble; the body cannot relax in the middle. It is almost as if an Olympic runner is getting ready, just waiting for the whistle, the signal, and he will be off, he will go like the wind. He is full of stress; now is no time to relax. If he takes a tranquilizer he will never be of any use in the race. Or if he relaxes and tries to do TM he will lose all. He has to use his stress: the stress is boiling, it is gathering energy. He is becoming more and more vital and potential. Now he has to sit on this stress and use it as energy, as fuel.

Selye has given this kind of stress a new name: he calls it *eustress,* like euphoria; it is a positive stress. After the runner has run he will fall into deep sleep; the problem has been solved. Now there is no problem, and the stress disappears of its own accord.

So also try this: when there is a stressful situation don't freak out, don't become afraid of it. Get into it, use it to fight with. A man has tremendous energy and the more you use it, the more you have of it.

Rolfing will be helpful also. It is not going to help you relax; it will simply change your musculature, it will make you more vital. So try Rolfing.

When stress comes and there is a situation, fight, do all that you can do, really go madly into it. Allow it, accept it, and welcome it. It is good; it prepares you to fight. And when you have worked it out, you will be surprised: great relaxation will come, and that relaxation is not created by you. Perhaps for two, three days you cannot sleep and then for forty-eight hours you can't wake up, and that is okay!

We carry around many wrong notions—for example, that every person has to sleep eight hours every day. It depends on the situation. There are situations when no sleep is needed: your house is on fire, and you are trying to sleep. Now that is not possible and should not be possible, otherwise who is going to put that fire out? And when the house is on fire, all other things are put aside; suddenly your body is ready to fight the fire. You will not feel sleepy. When the fire is gone and everything is settled, you may fall asleep for a long period, and that will do.

Everyone does not need the same amount of sleep either. A few people can do with three hours, two hours, four hours, five hours, or six, eight, ten, twelve hours. People differ; there is no norm. People also differ when it comes to stress.

There are two kinds of people in the world: one can be called the racehorse type and the other is the turtle type. If the racehorse type is not allowed to go fast, to go into things with speed, there will be stress; he has to be given his pace. And if you are a racehorse type, forget about relaxation and things like that; they are not for you. Those are for turtle type. So just be a racehorse—that is natural to you—and don't think of the joys that turtles are enjoying, because that is not for you. You enjoy a different kind of joy. If a turtle tries to become a racehorse he will have the same trouble!

You can get out of the marketplace. It is so easy; the mind will say, "Get out of the market, forget about it." But you will not feel good if you do; you will feel more stress arising because you will not feel that your energy is engaged.

So accept your nature. You are a fighter, a warrior; you have to be that way, and that's your joy. Now there is no need to be afraid; go into it wholeheartedly. Fight with the market, compete in the market, do all that you really want to do. Don't be afraid of the consequences; accept the stress. Once you accept the stress it will disappear. And not only that, you will feel very happy because you have started using the stress; it is a kind of energy.

If you are a racehorse type, don't listen to people who say to relax; that is not for you. Your relaxation will come only after you have earned it by hard labor. One has to understand one's type. Once you do there is no problem; then you can follow a clean-cut path. Stress is going to be your way of life.

[4] STRESS-RELATED ILLNESS

Question: *"I get sick very often and I think it has to do with pushing myself too much. Then I don't feel connected with my center any more and the body falls ill."*

Everybody has to understand his body's functioning. If you try to do something which is more than your body can tolerate, then sooner or later you will fall ill.

There is a certain limit to which you can push your body, but that cannot go on forever. You may be working too hard. It may not look too hard to other people, but that is not the point. Your body cannot tolerate that much; it has to rest. And the end result will be the same. Rather than working for two or three weeks and then resting for two or three weeks, work all six weeks but reduce the workload each day to half—simple arithmetic.

Pushing your body is very dangerous because it can destroy many fragile things in the body—being continuously overworked and then exhausted, depressed, and lying down in the bed and feeling bad about the whole thing is destructive. Reduce your speed, move slowly, and do it in an all-around way. For example, stop walking the way you walk. Walk slowly, breathe slowly, talk slowly. Eat slowly; if you take twenty minutes usually, take forty minutes now. Take your bath slowly; if you usually take ten minutes, take twenty minutes. And all activities should be reduced by half.

It is not only a question of your professional work. The whole twenty-four hours should be reduced, the speed at which everything is done should be cut by half. The whole life pattern and style has to change. Talk slowly, and even read slowly, because the mind tends to do everything in a particular way.

A person who is too much of a worker will read fast, talk fast, and eat fast; it is an obsession. Whatever he is doing, he will do at a fast pace, even when there is no need. If he has gone just for a morning walk, he will walk quickly. Going nowhere, just for a walk, and whether he goes two or three miles makes no difference. But a man obsessed with speed is always speedy. It is automatic; it is his automatic mechanical behavior.

So from today on, reduce everything to half. Stand slowly, walk slowly. And that will give you a deep awareness of things, because when you do things very slowly—for example, moving your hand—you become very aware of it. When you move it fast you do it mechanically.

If you want to slow down, you will have to slow down consciously; there is no other way.

It is not a question of capacity; it is simply a question of speed. Everybody has his own speed and you should move at your own speed. That is natural to you. It has nothing to do with capacity. You can do enough work with this much movement, and I think you will be able to do more. Once you come to your right rhythm, you will be able to do much more.

It will not be hectic, everything will run more smoothly, and you will be able to accomplish much more. There are slow workers, but this type of slowness results in its own kind of qualities. And in fact these are better qualities. A fast worker can be quantitatively good. He can produce more quantitatively, but qualitatively he can never be that good. A slow worker is qualitatively more perfect. His whole energy moves into a qualitative dimension. The quantity may not be much, but quantity is not the point really.

If you can do a few things, but really beautiful things, almost perfectly, you feel very happy and fulfilled. There is no need to do many things. If you can even do one thing that gives you total contentment, enough; your life is fulfilled. Or you can go on doing many things and nothing fulfills you and everything makes you nauseous and ill. What is the point of that?

A few basic things have to be understood. There is no such thing as human nature. There are as many human natures as there are human beings, so there is no criterion. Somebody is a fast runner, and another is a slow walker. They cannot be compared because both are separate, both are totally unique and individual. Do not be worried about that. Do not concern yourself with comparison. For example, you see that somebody is doing so much and never goes to bed and you do something and have to go to bed, and therefore you feel bad and think your capacity is not as much as it should be.

But who is he and how are you going to compare yourself to him? You are you, he is he. If he is forced to start moving slowly, he may get ill because that will be against his nature. What you are doing must be going against your nature—so just listen to your nature.

Always listen to your body. It whispers; it never shouts, because it cannot shout. Only in whispering does it give you messages. If you are alert, you will be able to understand them. And the body has a wisdom of its own, which is very much deeper than the mind. The mind is just immature. The body has remained without the mind for millennia. The mind is just a late arrival. It does not know much yet. All the basic things the body still keeps in its own control. Only useless things have been given to the mind— to think; to think about philosophy and God and hell and politics.

The most basic functions—breathing, digesting food, the circulation of blood—are under the control of the body, while only the luxuries are given to the mind.

So listen to your body, and never compare. Never before has there been a man like you and never will there be again. You are unique—past, present, future—so you cannot compare notes with anybody and you cannot imitate anybody.

[5] FEELING THE BODY FROM WITHIN

Question: *"I'm such a heady person, but recently my body and mind have been going through many changes. I've been feeling myself more from the inside, but now I'm afraid that I'm going to fall back into my old ways and that my mind is going to take back its control. How can I get more from the head into the body?"*

Whenever a change happens in the mind, the body is immediately affected. If it is a real change, you will always feel something deep down in the body also changing. And whenever something in the body is changing, there is no need to be afraid that the mind will take possession of you again; it is not easy. If only the mind changes and the body has not heard about it, then the mind can take possession very easily, because it remains on the surface. The body is where your roots are.

The body is where you are rooted in the earth, and the mind is just like branches in the sky—lovely to look at, but everything depends on the roots which are deep in the darkness of the earth. They don't exhibit themselves; they don't show. If you just move around you will see the branches and flowers, but you will never become aware of the roots.

If only the branches are changing and the roots have not been affected, that change is not going to last long. But if the roots are affected, then this change is going to last, and the process cannot be reversed easily. So don't be worried. Give more and more attention and feeling to the phenomenon that is happening to the body.

You are feeling inside the body—this is very beautiful. There are millions of people, almost the majority, who do not know any sense of the body. They have completely forgotten that they are in the body . . . they are just ghostlike.

To rediscover your own roots in the body is certainly a new sensation because humanity has been completely cut from the roots.

The body has been suppressed for millennia, and the mind has been given the idea that it is the master; that mind is all and the body is nothing but a servant, is in fact something condemnatory, is something like a sin.

One feels embarrassed that one has a body. That's why people are afraid of being naked, because once you are naked, you are more of a body than a mind. Clothes give you a feeling that the body doesn't exist—just the face, the head, the eyes. The whole mechanism of the mind is located there. So when they are naked, people suddenly feel that they are bodies—and that doesn't feel good.

Remain inside your body because that is the reality. Feel more and more . . . Allow your body to have all the sensitivity it can have. Regain it, reclaim it, and allow your body more changes so that you can feel its being. For example, sometimes close your eyes and lie down on the earth, feel the earth with your body. Don't think about it, feel it.

Go into the river and lie down in the water, in the sand. Just lie in the sun. Feel more . . . be sensuous. When you eat bread, first feel it with your hand, put it on your cheek and feel it, smell it. First let it be known by your body. Then taste it . . . Close your eyes and let the taste spread all over. And don't be in a hurry; don't simply go on stuffing it in. Enjoy it, chew it well—because this bread is going to become your body. Don't miss this opportunity. This bread is your potential body. So receive it, welcome it, and you will have a totally different body within a few months.

If you eat with a different mind, a different attitude; drink water with a different attitude, and remember always to be more sensuous, sensitive, soon you will see that your body has been dead in many parts. You become alive, as if you were a lion sleeping and now the lion is coming back, spreading its legs, stretching its body. You will find that same sensation of arising life. It is almost a resurrection.

[6] SLEEPLESSNESS

Question: *"I don't sleep well and I always wake up between three and four in the morning."*

You always get up between three and four? Then make that a meditation time.

Always use opportunities for some positive good. Be creative about everything. If you cannot sleep, then there is no need to force sleep, for sleep cannot be forced in the first place. Sleep is one of those energies that cannot be willed. If you will it, you will be disturbed. If you do something to try to force sleep, your very doing will be the hindrance, because sleep is against doing; it is a state of non-doing. So if you make any effort—for example if you start counting sheep or you start repeating a mantra or you start turning this way and that, or you start calling out for God and start praying—all that will make you more awake. It won't help but that's what people go on doing.

My approach is totally different. First, if sleep is gone that

simply means your body is perfectly rested and people have different needs . . .

"But I feel exhausted."

That is your mind; that has nothing to do with your body. Just
the idea that you have not been sleeping well tires you. It is not really the lack of sleep, because the body mechanism, the body organism, has its own wisdom. For example, you are eating, and the
body says, "Enough!" but you say, "Because I am so thin and lean, I
have to eat more." That is wrong; you are creating trouble for
yourself. You can eat, you can force a little more, you can stuff, but
the organism is not ready for it and it will reject the food.

One day you are not feeling like eating at all, but your mind
says that if you don't eat you will become weak. Nobody becomes
weak in one day. If your body is not feeling like eating, it is better
to listen to it; it knows better. It has an instinctive knowledge that
at this moment eating will be dangerous. Maybe some work is going on in the intestines and the body wants to clean it before you
put in any more food. Maybe some poison has entered. You have
already taken in too much food and the body has not been able to
finish its work with it. It does not need any more work; otherwise
the whole mechanism will go berserk; it will not be possible for it
to manage. So the body says, "No food, no appetite." No appetite
is body language, just a symbol for you. The body cannot speak
verbally: it cannot say, "Stop!" That is a symbol, a body symbol: no
appetite. The body is saying, "Don't eat!" but you in your mind
feel that you have to eat at least twice or three times a day, otherwise you will become weak. So you go on stuffing yourself, and because you have no appetite you try to create a false appetite. You
will put more spices in the food to create a false appetite or you
will go to someplace where you always like to eat. You are trying
to deceive the body, but this is just stupid!

And the same happens with sleep. If you have fallen asleep and at three or four you feel you are wakeful, that simply means the body is rested. The body's sleep is finished, now your mind is creating trouble. So use that hour. Just lie down there silently; enjoy the silence of the night! Rather than getting disturbed because your sleep is broken, enjoy this moment for meditation. No need to get up: just lie there on the bed, rest, but listen . . . the sounds of the night are there, the silence of the night. The traffic noise is there but people are not there; everybody is asleep. This is beautiful! You are alone—almost as if you are in the mountains—with the darkness and the soothing quality of the darkness. Enjoy that and relax into that enjoyment.

You see the point? Otherwise you become miserable, that once again your sleep has been broken; again tomorrow you will be tired and worried and there will be tensions and anguish and anxiety. Those things will not allow you to go to sleep again.

Take a positive vision, use this time. Get in tune with the night, the sounds of the night, and enjoy! It has immense beauty. Then you will not know when you have fallen into sleep again . . . but that is a by-product, and that can only be a by-product. When you are so absorbed listening to the night sounds, again you will slip into sleep slowly—but not through any will.

And I am not saying that you have to meditate so that you can sleep, no. There is no "so that," there is no "therefore." I am simply saying to enjoy! And suddenly you will find that the sleep has happened. But whether it happens or not is irrelevant. If it happens, good; if it doesn't happen, also perfectly good. Just for three weeks do this and all tiredness will disappear. That is a mind thing. From the very morning you are carrying the idea that you are tired. Of course, you will be getting more and more tired. You will be afraid of everything, of every involvement.

You are already tired so if you do this you will be more tired. You are creating a neurosis around you.

Everyone has different needs for sleep and food. One person sleeps eight hours, another may need ten hours, and some may need only six and others may need even four, and sometimes there are people who need only three or two hours . . .

My own father could not sleep after three o'clock. He went to sleep at about eleven, so he had three, four hours' sleep at the most. My mother had always been worried, but I told my father to sit in meditation. So he sat from three, and that became his door to the divine. For years he sat from three to seven . . . and he almost became like a statue; he forgot his body.

That became the most precious experience of his life; no sleep could give it. He was fresh by three; that's how his mechanism, his body, was functioning. In the beginning he used to try to go to sleep. It was a misery because sleep wouldn't come and he would get tired trying to sleep; by morning he would be frustrated. If you struggle for three or four hours to sleep every night and sleep doesn't come, how can you not be frustrated? But after he found meditation, all the frustration disappeared, and those times became his most valuable moments. He started longing for them: for twenty-four hours he was thinking about them, because those were the most peaceful. He used the time rightly.

[7] TENSION AND RELAXATION

Question: *"I experience a lot of tension and stress. How can I relax more?"*

Start relaxing from the circumference—that's where we are, and we can start only from where we are. Relax the circumference of your being—relax your body, relax your behavior, relax your acts. Walk in a relaxed way, eat in a relaxed way, talk and listen in a relaxed way. Slow down every process. Don't be in a hurry and don't act in haste. Move as if all eternity is available to you—in fact, it is available to you. We are here from the beginning and we are going to be here to the very end, if there is a beginning and there is an end. In fact, there is no beginning and no end. We have always been here and we will be here always. Forms go on changing, but not the substance; garments go on changing, but not the soul.

Tension means hurry, fear, doubt. Tension means a constant effort to protect, to be secure, to be safe. Tension means preparing for the tomorrow now, or for the afterlife, afraid that tomorrow you will not be able to face the reality, so you have to prepare. Tension means the past that you have not lived really but only somehow bypassed; it hangs, it is a hangover, it surrounds you.

Remember one very fundamental thing about life: any experience that has not been lived will hang around you, will persist: "Finish me! Live me! Complete me!" There is an intrinsic quality in every experience that it tends and wants to be finished, completed. Once completed, it evaporates; incomplete, it persists, it tortures you, it haunts you, it attracts your attention. It says, "What are you going to do about me? I am still incomplete— fulfill me!"

Your whole past hangs around you with nothing completed— because nothing has been lived really, everything somehow bypassed, partially lived, only so-so, in a lukewarm way. There has been no intensity, no passion. You have been moving like a somnambulist, a sleepwalker. So that past hangs, and the future creates fear. And between the past and the future is crushed your present, the only reality.

You will have to relax from the circumference. The first step is to relax the body. Remember as often as possible to look in the

body, to find out if you have tension somewhere in your body—
at the neck, in the head, in the legs. If so, relax it consciously.
Just go to that part of the body, and persuade that part, say to it
lovingly, "Relax!"

And you will be surprised that if you approach any part of
your body, it listens, it follows you—it is your body! With
closed eyes, go inside your body from the toes to the head
searching for any place where there is a tension. And then talk to
that part as you would talk to a friend; let there be a dialogue between you and your body. Tell it to relax, and tell it, "There is
nothing to fear. Don't be afraid. I am here to take care—you can
relax." Slowly, slowly, you will learn the knack. Then your body
will become relaxed.

Then take another step, go a little deeper; tell your mind to
relax. And if your body listens, your mind also listens; but you
cannot start with the mind—you have to start at the beginning.
Many people start with the mind and they fail; they fail because
they start from the wrong place. Everything should be done in
the right order.

If you become capable of relaxing your body voluntarily,
then you will be able to help your mind relax voluntarily. The
mind is a more complex phenomenon. Once you have become
confident that your body listens to you, you will have a new trust
in yourself. Now even your mind can listen to you. It will take a
little longer with your mind, but it will happen.

When your mind is relaxed, then start relaxing your heart,
the world of your feelings and emotions—which is even more
complex, more subtle. But now you will be moving with trust,
with great trust in yourself. Now you will know it is possible. If it
is possible with the body and possible with the mind, it is possible
with the heart too. And only then, when you have gone through
these three steps, can you take the fourth step. Now you can go to

the innermost core of your being, which is beyond body, mind, and heart, you can go to the very center of your existence. And you will be able to relax it too.

And that relaxation certainly brings the greatest joy possible, the ultimate in ecstasy, acceptance. You will be full of bliss and rejoicing. Your life will have the quality of dance to it.

The whole of existence is dancing, except for man. The whole of existence proceeds in a very relaxed way, there is movement but it is utterly relaxed. Trees are growing and birds are chirping and rivers are flowing and stars are moving: everything is happening in a very relaxed way. No hurry, no haste, no worry, and no waste. Except for man. Man has fallen victim to his mind.

Man can rise above gods and fall below animals. Man has a great spectrum of possibilities. From the lowest to the highest, man is a ladder.

Start from the body, and then go, slowly, slowly, deeper. And don't start anything else unless you have solved the first problem. If your body is tense, don't start with your mind. Wait. Work on the body first. Remember, small things are of immense help.

You walk at a certain pace; that has become habitual, automatic. Now try to walk slowly. Buddha used to say to his disciples, "Walk very slowly, and take each step very consciously." If you take each step very consciously, you are bound to walk slowly. If you are running, hurrying, you will forget to do this. Hence Buddha walks very slowly.

Just try walking very slowly, and you will be surprised—a new quality of awareness will start happening in your body. Eat slowly, and you will find that there is great relaxation. Do everything slowly . . . Change the old patterns, leave behind the old habits.

First the body has to become utterly relaxed, like that of a small child, only then can you start with the mind. Move scientifically: first do the simplest, then the complex, finally the more complex. And only then can you relax at the ultimate core.

Relaxation is one of the most complex phenomena—very rich, multidimensional. All these things are part of it: let-go, trust, surrender, love, acceptance, going with the flow, union with existence, egolessness, ecstasy. All these are part of it, and all these start happening if you learn the ways of relaxation.

Your so-called religious beliefs have made you very tense, because they have created guilt in you. My effort here is to help you get rid of all guilt and all fear. Let me tell you, there is no hell and no heaven, so don't be afraid of hell and don't be greedy for heaven. All that exists is this moment. You can make this moment a hell or a heaven—that certainly is possible—but there is no heaven or hell somewhere else. Hell is when you are all tense, and heaven is when you are completely relaxed. Total relaxation is paradise.

[8] NEGATIVE FEELINGS ABOUT THE BODY

Question: *"I don't like myself, especially my body."*

If you have a certain idea about how the body should be, you will be miserable. The body is as it should be. This is the body you have; this is the body that God has given to you. Use it, enjoy it! And if you start loving it, you will find it changing, because if a person loves his body he starts taking care of it, and care encompasses everything. If you care, then you don't stuff it with unnecessary food. If you care, then you don't starve it. You listen to your body's demands, you listen to its hints—what it wants, when it wants it. When you care, when you love, you become attuned to your body, and your body automatically becomes okay. If you don't like your body, that will create a problem, because by and by you will become indifferent to your body and negligent of it because who cares about the enemy? You will not look at it; you will avoid it. You will stop listening to its messages, and then you will hate it more. But you are creating the whole problem. The body never creates problems; it is the mind that creates problems. Now, this is an idea of the mind. No animal has a problem about his body image, no animal, not even the hippopotamus! They are perfectly happy because there is no mind to create any negative thoughts; otherwise the hippopotamus might think, "Why am I like this?" Animals have no such problems.

Just drop the ideal. Love your body—this is your body, this is a gift from God. You have to enjoy it and you have to take care of it. When you take care, you exercise, you eat, and you sleep. You take every care because this is your instrument, just like your car, which you clean, which you listen to, listen to every hum, so you will know whether something is going wrong. You take care even if the body gets a scratch. Just take care of the body and it will be perfectly beautiful—it is! It is such a beautiful mechanism, and is so complex. It works so efficiently it goes on functioning for seventy years. Whether you are asleep or awake, aware or unaware, the body goes on functioning, and the functioning is so silent. Even without your caring it goes on functioning; it goes on doing service for you. One should be grateful to the body.

Just change your attitude and you will see that within six months your body has changed its form. It is almost like when you fall in love with a woman; you see that she immediately becomes beautiful. She may not have cared about her body up to this moment, but when a man falls in love with her, she starts taking care. She stands before the mirror for hours . . . because somebody loves her! The same happens when you love your body; you will see that your body starts changing. It is loved, it is taken care of, it is needed. It is a very delicate mechanism—people use it very crudely, violently. Just change your attitude and see the difference!

[9] PRETTY AND UNPRETTY

Question: *"I keep having this feeling that I am really ugly. Somehow I seem to be hypnotizing my friends and people I meet that it's not much fun looking at me."*

The mind goes on creating unnecessary problems. But that is the whole function of the mind—to create baseless problems. And once it creates them, you are caught up and you try to solve them. Don't try to solve them. Simply see the baselessness in them. The very irrelevance has to be seen, that's all. If you start doing something, then you have accepted the problem. Just see the irrelevance of it.

Every face is beautiful. Every face is differently beautiful. Every face is a separate face, and every face is unique. In fact, there is no comparison and no possibility of any comparison. If you accept this, you will become beautiful. Through acceptance, beauty happens. If you yourself deny and reject, then you will become crippled and ugly. Now there is a vicious circle.

First you reject; you don't accept—then you become ugly. Soon others will start feeling the ugliness, and you will say, "Right, so that's true. I was thinking along the right lines." So you reject yourself more. This is how the mind goes on fulfilling itself. And all its prophecies are bound to be fulfilled once you miss the first step. The first step is that you are you.

There is no criterion for beauty. In fact, for almost five thousand years philosophers have been trying to define beauty. And they have not been able to, because there is no criterion. One person is beautiful to someone and to another he is not. Even the most beautiful woman may seem ugly to someone. It is an absolutely personal choice.

So there is no criterion . . . and the criterion changes like fashions in clothes. For example, in India, if a woman does not have big breasts and big buttocks, she is not considered beautiful. Now in the West, buttocks are almost disappearing; breasts are also getting smaller and smaller. A different concept of beauty is arising.

And whatever the concept, the body fulfills it. It has to be understood that when big breasts are considered beautiful in a country, then women produce big breasts.

Ordinarily people say that novels, poetry, and literature reflect society. But it works the opposite way also. Novels, poetry, literature create society also. Once you have a certain idea that gets into people's minds, it works.

There is no criterion for who is beautiful and who is not. It is a personal liking; in fact, a whim. But if you don't accept yourself in the first place, you are creating a situation in which nobody can accept you. Because if you don't accept, you won't allow anybody else to accept you.

If you are a woman and a man falls in love with you, you will destroy that love, because you will say, "How can you fall in love with an ugly witch?" Or you will think the man has a very peculiar idea of beauty. If you don't love yourself, then no one else can love you either. So first everyone has to fall in love with himself.

Jesus says, "Love God. Love your neighbor like yourself." That is the basic precept. If you love yourself, then you can love your neighbor and you can love your God. But the basic commandment is: Love yourself.

If you love yourself, if you are happy with yourself, you will attract many people. A woman who loves herself must be beautiful, has to be beautiful. She creates beauty out of her love for herself. She becomes a grace, a dignity.

[10] FALSE AND TRUE BEAUTY

Question: *"What is beauty?"*

Inner beauty is the only beauty there is. All other beauties are only skin-deep. One can fool oneself for the time being, but sooner or later the other beauty wears out and one is left in utter ugliness because one never developed the real beauty. The real beauty has nothing to do with the face but with the luminosity that comes from within. It has nothing to do with the form of the eyes but rather with light that shines through them. It has nothing to do with the body but rather with the inner presence that vibrates through the body. Real beauty arises at the core of your being and spreads outward toward the body. False beauty is only on the surface; it has no roots in you, it is ungrounded.

Remember, one has to seek and search for the real beauty. And the real is eternal, it remains: once you have found it, you have found it forever. The momentary is simply a waste of time; it is a kind of dream. One can remain occupied in a dream for the time being, but as soon as you wake up you see that it was all foolish, stupid.

[11] AGING

Question: *"Help! I am getting old!"*

A very good feeling about one's own body helps life tremendously. It makes you more healthy, more whole. Many people have forgotten their bodies; they have become oblivious and they think the body is something that has to be hidden behind clothes, something that always has to be covered and not allowed to be seen; something obscene, impure. Absurd notions, neurotic notions.

The body is beautiful. The body as such is beautiful; young or old makes no difference. Of course youth has its own beauty and old age its own.

The young body is more vital. The old body is more wise. Each age has its own beauty; there is no need to compare them. And, particularly in the West, the old body has become a very frightening concept because life is somehow thought synonymous with youth, which is foolish. It is better in the East. Life there is seen more synonymous with the old, because an old man has lived more, experienced more, loved more; has known many seasons of life, ups and downs. The old man has lived youth. The youth has yet to live old age.

The old body simply carries all the experiences, the scars, the wounds, the grace that comes through ripening experiences. And once you start enjoying your body and loving it at whatever stage it is, suddenly you feel it is again beautiful, and that releases many things inside.

[12] FRIGIDITY

Question: *"I have a sexual problem . . . I feel there is something wrong with me, but I always pretend I enjoy sex with a man."*

One has to go beyond sex one day, but the way beyond goes through it, and if you never go into it rightly, it is very difficult to go beyond it. So going through it is part of going beyond. And people who cannot enjoy sex may have learned that attitude, may have been conditioned.

Around the world humanity is being corrupted by people—and the greatest corruption is that everybody is taught to feel guilty about enjoying themselves . . . as if something is wrong when you are happy. When you are miserable, everything is okay, but when you are happy, something is wrong. So happiness has been crushed and repressed—and unless you explode into happiness, you miss the whole opportunity of life.

Life exists for that purpose, one has to learn how to be absolutely happy, how to explode in it.

And certainly sex brings you the greatest possibility of explosion. It is one of the most natural ways to have a glimpse of *samadhi,* of deep meditation, of benediction. There are other ways to benediction but they are not as natural. Sex is the most natural way—it is biologically built-in. Sex is a gift of God so that any person—he may be religious, irreligious, Hindu, Mohammedan, may believe God exists, may not believe, be a communist, atheist, or whatever . . . But this one thing naturally gives a glimpse of something beyond—beyond the body, beyond the mind.

So, being a woman, there are three things you have to remember and try. First, when you are making love, be active. If you are inactive, this difficulty you feel can happen easily. When you are active, this will not happen so easily. Tell your boyfriend that he has to play the role of the woman and you will play the role of the man. Let it be a game. Let him be more passive and you become more active. When one is more active, the activity is more involved, your energy is more involved—it is difficult to stop it in the middle. But when you are passive you can stop any time because you are almost out of it. You are just like a spectator, so become more active instead. And this is just a temporary measure. Once you have attained orgasmic experience, then there is no need to continue—you can return to your old role of being a woman.

Now for the second thing: before you make love, dance together. Let it be a wild dance. Sing loudly, dance, play music if you want to. Have incense in the room. Make it an elaborate ritual . . . almost religious.

People don't move toward lovemaking in steps. Two persons are sitting, and suddenly they start making love. It is abrupt—especially for the woman. For the man it is not so abrupt because man's energy is different, and his sexuality is more local. A woman's sexuality is more total; her whole body has to be involved in it. So unless it is preceded by foreplay, a woman never gets deeply into it.

So first dance, sing, let the energy bubble up, and then be the active partner. And go wild! Don't have any pattern—just go wild. If you want to scream while making love, don't worry. If you want to sing, don't worry. If you want to just utter some gibberish, utter it—it will function like a mantra.

And finally, the third thing: every day from morning to evening, you have to take note of the other things in which you also must be repressing your joy. This has to be changed altogether. When you are eating, eat joyfully, because everything is interconnected. When you are dancing, joy has to be there. When meditating, be joyful. When talking to a person, be joyful, be radiant, flowing. When walking on the road, be joyful. Often we don't know how much we are missing. Just an ordinary walk along the road you bring you so much joy. Who knows? There may not be another day. Tomorrow you may not be able to walk along the road. Tomorrow you may not be there to receive the sun. The wind will be there, but you may not be. Who knows about tomorrow? This may be the last day, so always enjoy each moment of it as if it is going to be the last. Take the whole of it, squeeze it completely, don't leave anything in it. This way one lives intensely and passionately. And sex is just a byproduct of your total attitude, so you cannot just change your sexual experience. Everything is interconnected, and so you will have to change everything.

Eat joyously! Don't go on eating just to stuff the body—enjoy it! It is a sacrament. Walk, and enjoy it too. It is God's gift, and one has to be thankful for it. When talking to somebody, enjoy the conversation.

From this moment on also start enjoying things that on the surface have nothing to do with sex. The end result will be that if you enjoy other things, you will enjoy sex too. If you don't enjoy other things, you will not enjoy sex either.

It is my observation that the attitude toward sex is a very symbolic attitude; it shows everything about your whole life. So if you are not enjoying sex you will not be enjoying other things either, or you will be only enjoying them to a certain extent. A man who is afraid of happiness and joy is always afraid of many things.

Do these three things, and then report to me after three weeks. Enjoy three weeks of wild life. Forget all humanity—be an animal, pure animal, and then you can become a human being very easily. But to be an animal one needs to go deeply into things.

Unless you are a real animal, you cannot become a real human being. And unless you are a real human being, you cannot become a divine being.

Everything has a hierarchy: the animal is the base of the temple, humanity is the walls of the temple, and divinity is the roof. So the roof cannot exist without the base. One can have the roof, but if there are no walls, then it cannot exist either. Man is a three-story building: the first story is animal, the second is human, the third is divine. So start from the first, from the very beginning and lay down the foundation stone.

[13] IMPOTENCE

Question: *"Whenever I'm making love to a woman, this fear of impotence arises."*

The western attitude is always about making things happen, doing something! And there are a few things that cannot be "done." There the West becomes very crazy!

Sleep and sex—these are things you cannot "do," so the West suffers very much from lack of sleep, insomnia, and also from sex. Everyone is worried that he is not experiencing it as it should be. Orgasm does not come or it is very local or it is very lukewarm or it is not total. And the quality of sleep is not good: there are too many dreams. Many times one wakes or one has to wait hours for sleep to come. People are trying all kinds of things to bring sleep: tranquilizers, tricks, mantras, and Transcendental Meditation.

People are also very worried about sex. That very worry and that very effort to do something is the problem.

Sex happens; it is not a thing that you have to do. So you have to learn the eastern attitude toward sex, the Tantra attitude. The Tantra attitude is that you be loving to a person. There is no need to plan, there is no need to rehearse in the mind. There is no need to do anything in particular: just be loving and available. Go on playing with each other's energy. And when you start making love, there is no need to make it great. Otherwise you will be pretending and so will the other person. She will pretend that she is a great lover and you will pretend that you are a great lover . . . and both will be unsatisfied! There is no need to pose.

Making love is a very silent prayer. It is meditation. It is sacred; it is the holiest of holies. So while you are making love to a woman go very slowly, with taste, taking in every flavor of it. And go very slowly: there is no hurry, no need to hurry; there is enough time.

And while making love, forget about orgasm. Rather, be in a relaxed state with the woman, relax into each other. The western mind is continuously thinking about when it is coming and how to make it fast and great and this and that. That thinking does not allow the body energies to function. It does not allow the body to have its own way; the mind goes on interfering . . .

Relax with the other person. If nothing happens there is no need for anything to happen. If nothing happens, then that is what is happening . . . and that too is beautiful! Orgasm does not have to happen every day. Sex should be just being together, just dissolving into each other. Then one can keep making love for half an hour, for one hour, just relaxing into the other. Then you will be of utter mindlessness, because there is no need for the mind. Love is the only thing where the mind is not needed; and that's where the West is wrong: it brings in the mind even there!

So just relax into each other and forget about the mind. Enjoy the very presence of the other, the meeting, and get lost in it. Don't try to make anything out of it; there is nothing to make. Then one day there will be a valley orgasm; there will be no peak. There will be only relaxation, but that has its own peak because it has depth. Someday the body will trigger itself into a peak orgasm, but that will also be coming; you will just be there.

Sometimes there will be a valley, sometimes there will be a

peak . . . and that is a rhythm. You cannot have a peak every day. If you have only peaks, then the peak will not be very big. You have to earn the peak by going into the valley. So it is half and half. Sometimes it will be a valley orgasm. Then get lost in the darkness of the valley, the coolness and the peace. That is how you earn a peak. One day the energies are ready: they themselves are going toward the peak, not that you are taking them. How can you? Who are you and how can you manage to do it? By being in the valley the energy accumulates; the peak is born out of the valley. Then there is great orgasm; your whole being is suffused with joy.

In the peak it will be joy, in the valley it will be peace. Both are beautiful. And, finally, peace is more valuable than joy, because joy will be momentary: you cannot be on the peak for more than a moment. A peak means it is very small; it is like a pyramid. You cannot stand there for long; you can be there only for a moment. But you can be there longer when a valley comes. Both have to be enjoyed; both have something to deliver. Both are meaningful and both help you to grow.

Finally Tantra says the valley orgasm is far superior to the peak. The peak orgasm is immature, the valley orgasm has a great maturity in it. The peak orgasm has excitement; it is feverish, it is passionate. It has a thrill but that thrill is tiring. The valley orgasm has no thrill but it has silence, and that silence is far more valuable, far more transforming. That will remain with you for twenty-four hours. Once you have been in a valley that valley will follow you. The peak will be lost and you will be exhausted and will fall asleep. The valley will continue; for days it can have a kind of effect on you. You will feel relaxed, together.

Both are good, but nothing can be "done." One has simply to allow. So love is a kind of relaxation in which things have to be allowed.

[14] FEELING WITHDRAWN

Question: *"Sometimes I would like to hide myself in a dark hole, especially when I have my period."*

There are waves of energy. Sometimes it is a tide and sometimes it is the ebb. When you are in a tide it is very easy to relate, communicate, be open, to love, to receive, to give. When you are not in a tide and energy is ebbing, it is very difficult to communicate, almost impossible. But both come and go—they are both part of life. Nothing is wrong; it is natural—so remember to accept it.

When you feel that the ebb period is there, don't try to communicate. Don't force yourself to open because that opening will not be an opening. That is the seed time. One simply closes oneself and remains in oneself. Use that time for deep meditation. It is very fertile for meditation. When you are in a tide and energy is flowing and going higher, that is the time for love. Then relate, be open, share. That is the crop time, but it cannot be all year round. They say that even in heaven, angels don't sing all the time.

So when there is a song arising, sing. And when you feel that everything is closing, just help it to close. That's what being natural means. By being natural it is not meant that one should remain open for twenty-four hours—you are not a magical store. There are moments when one should close; otherwise it will be too tiring, too tedious, boring. There is no need to smile continuously—only politicians do that, and they are the most stupid people in the world.

There are times when tears are welcomed, and should be

welcomed. There are times when one feels sad—sadness is beautiful, so when you feel sad, be sad. When you feel happy, be happy. To be authentic means never be against that which is already happening. Go with it . . . trust it. In the night the petals of the lotus close, in the morning they open again—but that's a natural process.

Now in the modern mind—particularly in the new generation—a very wrong notion is arising, the notion that one has to be always open, that one has to be always loving. This is a new sort of torture, a new sort of repression, a new fashion in violence. There is no need for it. An authentic person is one who you can rely on. If he is sad, you can rely on the fact that he must be feeling sad; he is a true person. If he is closed, you can rely on that and you can trust him. It is a state of meditation—he wants just to be within himself. He does not want to go out; he is in deep introspection. Good! If he is smiling and talking, then he wants to relate and go out of his being and share. You can rely on such a person.

So don't try to enforce anything from your mind upon your being. Let the being have its say, and the mind should be just a follower, a servant. But the mind always tries to become the master. I don't see that anything is wrong. Just live this period and by and by you will see that every month it will be so. For a few days you will be very open—for a few days you will be closed.

It is more clear in women than in men because women still live in a periodicity. Because of their monthly course, their chemistry, the body chemistry goes in periods of twenty-eight days. In fact, the same happens to a man, but it is more subtle, more invisible.

Just recently a few researchers have revealed that there is a sort of monthly period for man also, but it is invisible because there is no release of blood. But as for four days of each month, a woman goes into a very low energy state, every man also goes into a low energy state for four days each month. This state in man is not so physical, not so visible; it is a psychic one—more inner than outer.

But if you track your moods you will be able to chart them. Note them on a calendar. My feeling is that you and your moods must be moving according to the moon, so just watch and relate how you go with the moon. Make a calendar for at least one or two months, and you will be able to predict your states. Then you can use it to plan your life.

If you want to meet friends, never meet them when you are closed; meet them when you are open. But there is nothing wrong with this, it is just a natural process.

[15] HYPOCHONDRIA

Question: *"I am constantly worrying about my body, that it will fall sick. Can you give me some advice?"*

If you think too much about your body, the body becomes ill, and when the body becomes ill, naturally you think about it more. It becomes a vicious cycle.

Even if a healthy person, a perfectly healthy person, starts thinking about his stomach—how he is going to digest this and that and what is going to happen—within twenty-four hours his stomach will be disturbed. And once it is disturbed, he will think about it more. So nothing is basically wrong with the body, it is just that an idea has disturbed it. Medicine can't help because medicine can't cure the idea. Therefore you can go from one doctor to another, from one "pathy" to another "pathy" and none will be much help. Their treatments may even disturb you further because the medicines will have an effect but they will not cure the idea. And there is no other disease except the idea.

And the more you fail with the doctors, the more you become concerned with your body. Then a body-consciousness arises. You become very touchy about your body. Just a slight change, slight difficulty, slight discomfort, and you get into a panic. Then panic helps the body to become more and more disturbed.

So my first suggestion is that you drop the idea that something is wrong. Start living.

It happened once. . . .

A man was told by a doctor that he would not live more than six months. That man had been ill for twenty years with a thousand and one kinds of illnesses. All that can happen to a human being was happening to him. The doctors were tired; and he was very rich. He was a hypochondriac, and just out of sheer tiredness the doctor said, "You cannot survive, so forget about it. Six months more and you will die; that is certain. Now nobody can save you. So if you want to live, you can live for six months."

The man thought, If I am going to live only for six months then why bother about the body? It is going to die. So for the first time he shifted his consciousness. He ordered the best clothes, he purchased the best cars, and he planned a world tour. He went to every place that he always wanted to go to but had not gone because of his body. He traveled around the world, ate everything that he always wanted to eat, made love to women, purchased everything that he wanted . . . really lived! Death was coming so there was no point in holding back. After six months when he went back, he was healthier than he had ever been before. He lived thirty years more and the problem never came up again!

You have to drop that consciousness. Naturopathy is good, for example, because it is not a true "pathy"; it is just a rest. But don't become a faddist, because that is an illness. Naturopathy in itself is not a "pathy"; it is just giving rest to the body, giving the body a situation in which it can become attuned to nature. It is an attuning with the instinctive nature; it is nonmedicinal. But the danger with Naturopathy is that it can become a fad, and the fad is more problematic than the disease. Naturopathy helps many people, but it is very rare that a person who has been helped by Naturopathy does not become ill with Naturopathy itself. The person becomes obsessed: he constantly thinks about what to eat, and what not to eat, where to go, and where not to go, and about ecology and all like that. When this happens, life becomes difficult again. If you become obsessed with Naturopathy you cannot breathe because there is so much pollution in the air. You cannot eat in a restaurant because meals are not prepared in a natural way. You cannot eat this thing or that thing, because you would like only natural foods. You cannot live in a city. The result is that life becomes really difficult.

Always remember, Naturopathy is just a rest. Once in a while, even for no reason, one should go to a Naturopathy clinic and rest for two, three weeks, one month, two months, for as long as one can afford every year. Go for no particular reason, just to enjoy nature and natural foods and baths and saunas and massage. Go just for simple joy, the sheer joy of the experience. But drop the idea that you are ill. And think of the inner king; the body is just a palace.

[16] ENLIVENING THE SENSES

Question: *"I do intellectual work and I spend most of my time at the computer. I often feel so unalive."*

Get more into your body. Make your senses more alive. See more lovingly, taste more lovingly, touch more lovingly, smell more lovingly. Let your senses function more and more. Then suddenly you will see the energy that was moving too much in the head is now well dispersed in the body.

The head is very dictatorial. It goes on taking energy from everywhere and is a monopolist. It has killed your senses. Your head is taking almost 80 percent of the energy, and only 20 percent is left for the rest of the body. Of course the whole body suffers, and when the whole body suffers, you suffer, because you can only be happy when you are functioning as a whole, as an organic unity, and every part of your body and being is getting its proper portion of energy—not more than that, not less. Then you function in a rhythm; you have a harmony.

Harmony, happiness, health—they are all part of one phenomenon, and that is wholeness. If you are whole, you are happy, healthy, harmonious.

The head is creating a disturbance. People have lost many things. They cannot smell because have lost the capacity to smell. They have lost the capacity to taste. They can only hear a few things because they have lost the function of their ears. People don't know what touch really is. Their skin has become dead. It has lost its softness and receptivity. So the head thrives like an Adolf Hitler, crushing the whole body. The head becomes bigger and bigger. It is ridiculous. Man becomes almost a caricature—a very large head and very small limbs, hanging.

So bring back your senses. Do anything with your hands, with the earth, with the trees, with the rocks, with bodies, with people. Do anything that does not require much thinking, not much intellectualization. And enjoy. Then your head will by and by be unburdened. It will be good for your head too, because when the head is burdened too much, it thinks—but it cannot think. How can a worrying mind think? For thinking you need clarity. For thinking you need a non-tense mind.

It may seem like a paradox, but for thinking you need a thoughtless mind. Then you can think very easily, very directly, intensely. Just put any problem before yourself and your non-thinking mind starts solving it. Then you have intuition. It is not worry—just insight.

When the mind is burdened too much with thoughts, you think too much but to no purpose. It comes to nothing; there is nothing in your head. You go round and round; you make much noise, but the net result is zero.

So it is not against the head to disperse the energy into all the senses. It is in favor of it, because when the head is balanced, in its right place, it functions better; otherwise it is jammed up. There is such great traffic in it, it is almost like a rush hour, a continuous, twenty-four-hour rush hour.

The body is beautiful. Anything to do with the body is beautiful.

[17] SENSUOUSNESS

Question: *"What is sensuousness?"*

Sensuousness means you are open, your doors are open, you are ready to throb with existence. If a bird starts singing, the sensuous person immediately feels the song echoed in his deepest core of being. The nonsensuous person does not hear it at all, or maybe just as a noise somewhere; it does not penetrate his heart. A cuckoo starts calling—a sensuous person starts feeling as if the cuckoo is not calling from some faraway mango grove but from deep down within his own soul. It becomes his own call, it becomes his own longing for the divine, his own longing for the beloved. In that moment the observer and the observed are one. Seeing a beautiful flower bloom, the sensuous person blooms with it, becomes a flower with it.

The sensuous person is liquid, flowing, fluid. Each experience, and he becomes it. Seeing a sunset, he is the sunset. Seeing a night, a dark night, beautiful silent darkness, he becomes the darkness. In the morning he becomes the light.

He is all that life is. He tastes life from every nook and corner. Hence he becomes rich; this is real richness. Listening to music he is music; listening to the sound of water he becomes that sound. And when the wind passes through a bamboo grove, and the cracking bamboos, he is not far away from them. He is amidst them, one of them—he is a bamboo.

A Zen master told one of his disciples who wanted to paint bamboos, "Go and first become a bamboo." He was an accomplished painter, he had passed all the art examinations, and with distinction. His name had already started becoming famous. And the Master said, "You go to the forest, live with the bamboos for a few years, become a bamboo. And the day you can become a bamboo, come back and paint, not before it. How can you paint a bamboo if you have not known what a bamboo feels like from within? You can paint a bamboo from the outside, but that is just a photograph."

And that is the difference between photography and painting.

A photograph can never be a painting. However skillfully, artfully done, it remains only the reflection of the circumference of the bamboo. No camera can enter into the soul.

When at first photography was developed, a great fear arose in the world of painting that maybe now painting would lose its old beauty and its old pedestal; because photography would be developed more and more every day and soon it would fulfill its requirement. That fear was proved baseless. In fact, after the invention of the camera, photography developed tremendously, but simultaneously painting has learned new dimensions, new visions, new perceptions. Painting has become richer; it had to. Before the invention of the camera the painter was functioning as a camera.

The Master said, "You go to the forest." And the disciple went, and for three years he remained in the forest, being with the bamboos in all kinds of climates. Because when it is raining the bamboo has one joy, and when it is windy the bamboo has a different mood, and when it is sunny, of course everything changes in the being of the bamboo. And when a cuckoo comes into the bamboo grove and starts calling, the bamboos are silent and responsive. The disciple had to remain there for three years.

And then it happened, one day it happened: sitting by the side of the bamboos, he forgot who he was. And the wind started blowing and he started swaying—like a bamboo! Only later on did he remember that for a long time he had not been a man. He had entered into the soul of the bamboo, then he painted the bamboos.

Those bamboos certainly have a totally different quality that no photograph can capture. Photographs can be beautiful, but they are dead. That particular painting is alive because it shows the soul of the bamboo in all its moods, in all its richness, in all its climates. Sadness is there, joy is there, agony is there, and ecstasy is there, and all that a bamboo knows, the whole biography of a bamboo is there.

To be sensuous is to be available to the mysteries of life. Become more and more sensuous, and drop all condemnation. Let your body become just a door.

[18] TOO MUCH FOOD, TOO LITTLE SEX

Question: *"Since my relationship broke up I have been eating too much and getting fat. How can I regain my balance and eat less?"*

Whenever you don't allow sex energy to move in the right direction it starts getting obsessed with food. Food and sex are polarities; they balance each other. If you have too much sex, your interest in food will disappear. If repress your sexuality, your interest in food will become almost obsessive. So you cannot do anything directly about your food, and if you try to, you will be in constant trouble. For a few days you can force yourself manage, but then the problem will return, and it will return with a vengeance. You will have to work on your sexual energy.

The problem arises because the first experiences of food and love for the child are very deeply connected. He gets food from his mother's breast and love too. When the child gets love he is not worried about milk; his mother has to persuade him. If the child is not getting love, then he does not leave the breast, because he is afraid about the future. He has to drink as much as he can because he cannot be certain when his mother will be available. If the child gets love, he is secure; he does not worry. Whenever there is need his mother will be available; he can trust her love. But if a mother is not loving then the child cannot trust; then he has to drink as much as he can. He goes on overeating.

So if a child does not get love he becomes interested in food;

if he gets love he is not interested in food, or has just a natural interest—he takes just as much as is needed by the body.

If somehow you have been blocking your love energy, that blocked love energy will become your interest in food. If you want to change it, you will have to move into love a little more, you will have to become more loving. Love your own body. Begin from there; enjoy your own body. It is a beautiful phenomenon; it is such a gift. Dance, sing, feel, and touch your own body.

The problem is that if you don't love your own body, you will not allow anybody else to love your body either. In fact, the person who tries to be loving toward you will look ridiculous, foolish, stupid. Because you cannot love your body, you wonder what is it he sees in you? You don't see anything! Unless you start seeing the beauty of your own body, you will not be able to accept somebody else's love. The very idea that a person is loving toward you shows that he is stupid and nothing else.

So I say, be loving to your body. And if any opportunity arises where you can be loving, hugging, holding hands, don't miss it. You will be surprised: as you start moving into love the food problem will be solved automatically. To be in love is a great experience and to go on stuffing food in yourself is a very miserable experience—not that food is not beautiful, but food is beautiful only when taken in quantities that you can absorb. When you take too much it is nauseating.

There is something beautiful about love: it is never too much. Nobody can love to the extreme, nobody; there is no extreme. Unlike when you eat to extreme, you stuff things in; when you love, you share, you give. It is an unburdening phenomenon. And the more you give, the more your energy starts flowing. You become a river, no more a stagnant pool.

That is what you have done: you have made your energy a stagnant pool.

Break the walls! You are unnecessarily missing something beautiful that love and only love can bring, and instead you are suffering with this problem of food.

[19] DETOXIFICATION THROUGH FASTING

Question: *"Do you recommend fasting as a method for detoxifying the body? I have started to become a vegetarian recently."*

Whenever you are on a fast the body has no more work of digestion. In that period the body can work at throwing out dead cells, toxins. It is just as one day, Sunday or Saturday, you are on a holiday and you come home and you clean all day long. The whole week you were so engaged and so busy you couldn't clean the house, so you are doing it all on one day. When the body has nothing to digest, when you have not eaten anything, the body starts a self-cleaning. A process starts spontaneously and the body starts throwing out all that is not needed, all that feels like a load. Fasting is a method of purification. Once in a while, a fast is beautiful—not doing anything, not eating, just resting. Take as much liquid as possible and just rest, and the body will be cleaned.

Sometimes, if you feel that a longer fast is needed, you can do a longer fast also—but be deep in love with your body while you are doing it. And if you feel the fast is harming your body in any way, stop it. If the fast is helping your body, you will feel more energetic; you will feel more alive; you will feel rejuvenated and vitalized. This should be the criterion: if you start feeling that you are getting weaker, if you start feeling that a subtle trembling is coming into the body, then be aware—now the fast is no longer a purification; it has become destructive. Stop it.

But one should learn the whole science of fasting first. In

fact, before fasting one should consult somebody who has been fasting for a long time and who knows the whole path very well, who knows all the symptoms of problems: if it becomes destructive, what will start happening; if it is not destructive, then what will happen. After a real, purifying fast you will feel new, younger, cleaner, weightless, happier; and the body will be functioning better because now it is unloaded. But you should fast only if you have been eating wrongly. If you have not been eating wrongly, there is no need to fast. Fasting is needed only when you have already abused the body by your eating habits—and we all have been doing that.

Man has lost the path. No animal eats like man; every animal has its chosen food. If you bring buffaloes in the garden and leave them, they will eat only a particular grass. They will not go on eating everything and anything—they are very choosy. They have a certain feeling about their food. Man is completely lost, has no feeling about his food. He goes on eating everything and anything. In fact, you cannot find anything that is not eaten somewhere or other by man. In some places, ants are eaten. In some places, snakes are eaten. In some places, dogs are eaten. Man has eaten everything. Man is simply mad. He does not know what is in resonance with his body and what is not. He is completely confused.

Man, naturally, should be a vegetarian, because the whole body is made for vegetarian food. Even scientists concede to the fact that the whole structure of the human body shows that man should be a vegetarian. Man is descended from the monkeys. Monkeys are vegetarians—total vegetarians. If Darwin's concept is true, then man should be a vegetarian. Now there are ways to ascertain whether a certain species of animal is vegetarian or nonvegetarian: it depends on the intestine, the length of the intestine. Nonvegetarian animals have a very small intestine.

Tigers, lions—they have a very small intestine, because meat is already a digested food. It does not need a long intestine to digest it. The work of digestion has been done by the animal. Now you are eating the animal's meat. It is already digested—no long intestine is needed. Man has one of the longest intestines: that means man is a vegetarian. A long digestion is needed, and much excreta will be there that has to be expelled.

If man is a vegetarian and he goes on eating meat, the body is burdened. In the East, all the great meditators—Buddha, Mahavir—have emphasized that fact. This is not due to any concept of nonviolence—that is a secondary thing—but because if you really want to move in deep meditation your body needs to be weightless, natural, flowing. Your body needs to be unloaded; and a nonvegetarian's body is very much loaded.

Just watch what happens when you eat meat. When you kill an animal, what happens to the animal when he is killed? Of course, nobody wants to be killed. Life wants to prolong itself; the animal is not dying willingly. If somebody kills you, you will not die willingly. If a lion jumps on you and kills you, what will happen to your mind? The same happens when you kill a lion. Agony, fear, death, anguish, anxiety, anger, violence, sadness— all these things happen to the animal. All over his body violence, anguish, agony spreads. The whole body becomes full of toxins, poisons. All the body glands release poisons because the animal is dying very unwillingly. And then you eat the meat—that meat carries all the poisons that the animal has released. The whole energy is poisonous. Those poisons are then carried in your body.

And that meat which you are eating belonged to an animal body. It had a specific purpose there. A specific type of consciousness existed in the animal's body. You are on a higher plane than the animal's consciousness, and when you eat the animal's meat your body goes to the lowest plane, to the lower plane of the animal. Then there exists a gap between your consciousness and your body, and a tension arises, and anxiety arises.

One should eat things that are natural—natural for you. Fruits, nuts, vegetables—eat as much as you can. And the beauty is that you cannot eat more of these things than is needed. Whatever is natural always gives you satisfaction, because it satiates your body, saturates you. You feel fulfilled. If some thing is unnatural it never gives you a feeling of fulfillment. Go on eating ice cream: you will never feel that you are satiated. In fact, the more you eat, the more you feel like eating. It is not a food. Your mind is being tricked. Now you are not eating according to your body's need; you are eating just to taste the ice cream. The tongue has become the controller.

The tongue should not be the controller. It does not know anything about the stomach. It does not know anything about the body. The tongue has a specific purpose to fulfill: to taste food. Naturally, the tongue has to judge—that is its only function— which food is for the body—for my body—and which food is not. It is just a watchman at the door; it is not the master. And if the watchman at the door becomes the master, then everything becomes confused.

[20] FASTING AND FEASTING

If sometimes you feel that a fast comes naturally—not as a law, not as a principle, not as a philosophy to be followed, as a discipline to be imposed, but out of your natural desire for it—it is good. Then, too, remember always that your fast is in the service of feasting, so that you can eat well again. The purpose of fasting is as a means, never as an end; and that will happen rarely, once in a while. And if you are perfectly aware while you are eating, and enjoying it, you will never eat too much.

My insistence is not on dieting but on awareness. Eat well, enjoy it to the fullest. Remember, the rule is that if you don't enjoy your food you will have to eat more to compensate. If you enjoy your food, you will eat less, and there will be no need to compensate. If you eat slowly, tasting every bit of it, chewing well, you are completely absorbed into it. Eating should be a meditation.

I am not against taste because I am not against the senses. To be sensitive is to be intelligent, to be sensitive is to be alive. Your so-called religions have tried to desensitize you, to make you dull. They are against taste; they would like you to make your tongue absolutely dull so you don't taste anything. But that is not a state of health; the tongue becomes dull only in illness. When you have a fever, the tongue becomes dull. When you are healthy the tongue is sensitive; it is alive, throbbing, pulsates with energy. I am not against taste, I am for taste. Eat well, taste well; taste is divine.

And so, exactly like taste, you have to look at beauty and enjoy it; you have to listen to music and enjoy it; you have to touch the rocks and leaves and human beings—their warmth, their texture—and enjoy them. Use all your senses, use them at their optimum, then you will really live and your life will be aflame; it will not be dull, it will be aflame with energy and vitality. I am not in favor of those people who have been teaching you to kill your senses, they are against the body.

And remember, the body is your temple, the body is a divine gift. It is so delicate and so beautiful and so wonderful—to kill it is to be ungrateful to God. God has given you taste; you have not created it, it is not anything to do with you. God has given you eyes and has made this psychedelic world so colorful, and he has given you eyes. Let there be a great communion between the eyes and the colors of the world. And he has made everything and there is a tremendous harmony. Don't break this harmony.

Listen to your body. The body is not your enemy, and when the body is saying something, do accordingly, because the body has a wisdom of its own. Don't disturb it, don't go on a mind-trip. That's why I don't teach dieting, I teach only awareness. Eat with full awareness, eat meditatively, and then you will never eat too much and you will never eat too little. Too much is as bad as too little; these are extremes. Nature wants you to be balanced, to be in a sort of equilibrium, to be in the middle, neither less nor more. Don't go to the extreme. To go to the extreme is to be neurotic.

There are two types of neurotics about food: those who go on eating, not listening to the body—the body goes on crying and screaming "Stop!" and they go on; and then there is the other variety—the body goes on screaming "I am hungry!" and they are on a fast. Both are neurotic, both are pathological. All need treatment, all need to be hospitalized. Because a healthy person is one who is balanced: in whatever he is doing, he is always in the middle. He never goes to any extreme because all extremes will create tensions and anxieties. When you eat too much, there is anxiety because the body is burdened. When you don't eat enough, then there is anxiety because the body is hungry. A healthy person is one who knows when to stop; and that should come out of your awareness, not out of a certain teaching.

If I tell you how much to eat, that is going to be dangerous because it will be just an average. Some people are very thin and some are very fat, and if I tell you how much to eat—"three chapatis"—then for some it may be too much and for some it may be not enough. So I don't teach rigid rules, I simply give you a sense of awareness.

Listen to your body: you have a unique body. And remember there are different types of energies, different types of involvement. One person is a professor in a university; he does not exert much energy as far as his body is concerned; he will not need much food, and he will need a different kind of food. Another person is a laborer; he will need much food, and a different kind of food. A rigid principle for eating would be dangerous. No rule can be given as a universal rule.

George Bernard Shaw has said that there is only one golden rule, that there are no golden rules. Remember that there is no golden rule—there cannot be, because each individual is so unique that nobody can prescribe. So I simply give you a sense. And my sense is not of principles, of laws; my approach is of awareness, because today you may need more food and tomorrow you may not need that much. It is not only a question of you being different from others—every day of your life is different from every other day. Today you have rested all day, and you may not need much food. Another day you have been in the garden digging the hole all day, and you may need much food. One just should be alert and one should be capable of listening to what the body is saying. Go according to the body.

Neither is the body the master, nor is the body the slave; the body is your friend—befriend your body. The one who goes on eating too much and the one who goes on dieting are both in the same trap. They are both deaf; they don't listen to what the body is saying.

And it is nonsense that it is a sin to eat for the benefit of the tongue. Then for what will you eat? If it is a sin to see for the eye, for what will you see? If it is a sin to hear for the ear, then for what will you hear? Then there is nothing left for you—commit suicide, because the whole of life is of the senses. Whatever you do, the senses come in. It is through the senses that you flow and relate with life. When you eat with taste, God inside is fulfilled, satisfied; and when you eat with taste, the God within food is respected.

But your mahatmas, your so-called religious gurus have been teaching self-torture. In the name of religion they have been simply teaching nothing but masochism: "Torture yourself. The more you torture yourself, the more valuable you become in the eyes of God. The more unhappy you are, the more virtue you have. If you are happy, you commit sin. Happiness is sin; to be unhappy is to be virtuous." This is their logic.

I cannot see the point; it is so absurd, so illogical, so patently foolish. God is happy, so if you want to be in tune with God be happy. This is my teaching: God is happy, so if you want to be in tune with God be happy, because whenever you are happy, you fall in step with God; whenever you are unhappy, you are out of step. A miserable man cannot be a religious man.

If you ask me what is sin—I say there is only one sin: to be miserable is to be a sinner. To be happy, really happy, is to be a saint. Let your religion teach you how to sing and how to dance and how to delight in life. Let your religion be an affirmative religion, a yea-saying religion, a religion of happiness, joy, bliss. Throw away all the nonsense that you have been carrying around for centuries, that has crippled the whole of humanity. This nonsense has made people so ugly and so unhappy and so miserable. And it appeals only to the pathological—those who want to torture themselves, for it gives them an excuse.

To torture oneself or to torture others, both are diseases—

the very idea to torture is sick. If somebody is an Adolf Hitler, he tortures others; if somebody is a Mahatma Gandhi, he tortures himself. Both are in the same boat—they may be standing back to back, but they are standing in the same boat. Adolf Hitler's joy was in torturing others, Mahatma Gandhi's joy was in torturing himself, but both are violent. The logic is the same—their joy depends on torture. Their direction is different, but the direction is not the question; their mind has the same attitude: torture. You respect a person who tortures himself because you don't understand the logic of it. Adolf Hitler is condemned around the world and Gandhi is worshipped, and I am simply puzzled. How is it possible?—because the logic is the same. Gandhi says, "Don't eat anything for taste. Taste should not be allowed. Eat as a duty, not as a joy. Eat because one has to live, that's all." He reduces the joy of eating to the ordinary world of work: "Don't eat as play." Remember, animals eat that way. They eat just to eat, just to exist, to survive. Have you seen animals enjoying food? Not at all. They don't have feasts and parties, and they don't sing and dance. Only man has made eating a great feast.

And the attitude is the same about other things. Gandhi says, "Make love only if you want a child, otherwise never. Let love be only biological. Eating should be only to survive and love should be so that the race survives. Never make love as fun."

That's what animals do. Have you looked at a dog making love? Look in his face, you will not find any fun . . . just a sort of duty. He has to do it, something is enforced from within—the biological urge. And the moment he has made love, he forgets the beloved, he goes on his own way, he never says even a thank you. Finished, the job is done! Only man makes love for fun. That is where humanity is higher than animals—only man makes love for fun; just for the joy of it, just for the beauty of it, just for the music and the poetry of it.

That's why I say the pill is one of the greatest revolutions in the world because it has completely changed the whole concept of love. Now one can love only for joy. There is no need to be under biological slavery, there is no need to make love only when you want a child. Now sex and love are completely separate. The pill brought about the greatest revolution: now sex is sex and love is love. Sex is when it is biological; love is when it is simply the beautiful music of two bodies meeting, engulfing each other, disappearing into each other, losing into each other, falling into a totally new dimension of rhythm, harmony . . . an orgasmic experience. No problem of children, no biological push-pull, nothing. Now the act in itself is beautiful, no more a means toward any end—that is the difference. Work is when it is a means to some end. Play is when the end and the means are together. Play is when the means itself is the end—there is no other end to it.

Eat for the joy of it; then you are human, a higher being. Love for the joy of love; then you are a higher being. Listen for the joy of listening and you will be freed from the confinement of instincts.

I am not against happiness, I am all for it. I am a hedonist, and this is my understanding: that all the great spiritual people of the world have always been hedonists. If somebody is not a hedonist and pretends to be a spiritual person, he is not—he is a psychopath. Because happiness is the very goal, the very source, the very end of all things. God is seeking happiness through you, in millions of forms. Allow him all the happiness that is possible and help him to go to higher peaks, higher reaches, of happiness. Then you are religious, and then your temples will become places of celebration and your churches will not be so sad and ugly, so somber, so dead, like graveyards. Then there will be laughter and there will be song and there will be dance and there will be great rejoicing.

The essential religion is nothing but joy. So whatever gives you joy is virtuous; whatsoever makes you sad, unhappy, miserable is a sin. Let that be the criterion.

I don't give rigid rules because I know how the human mind functions. Once a rigid rule is given, you forget awareness and you start following that rule. A rigid rule is not the question— you can follow the rule and you will never grow.

Listen to a few anecdotes:

> Benny arrived home to find the kitchen a mess of broken crockery.
>
> "What happened?" he asked his wife.
>
> "There's something wrong with this cookbook," she explained. "It says that an old cup without a handle will do for the measuring—and it's taken me eleven tries to get a handle off without breaking the cup."

Now if the cookbook says that, it has to be done. The human mind is foolish—remember it. Once you have a rigid rule, you follow it.

> The mob was meeting the big guy, and what the big guy said, went. The buzzer rang and the servant went over to answer the door. He peeked through the slot in the frame, and, recognizing the visitor, allowed the panel to swing back.
>
> "Leave your umbrella at the door," the servant told the visitor.
>
> "I ain't got one," answered the visitor.

"Then get back home and get one. The boss told me everyone must leave their umbrella at the door. Otherwise I am not going to allow you in."

A rule is a rule.

It was a desperate chase but the police car was catching up to the bank robbers when suddenly it swerved into a gas station, from which point the cop driving phoned his chief.

"Did you catch them?" the chief asked excitedly.

"They were lucky," replied the cop. "We were closing the gap, only half a mile away, when I noticed our five hundred miles were up and we had to stop and change our oil."

What can you do when the oil has to be changed after each five hundred miles and five hundred miles are up? You have to change the oil first.

I never give you rigid rules because I know how stupid the human mind is and can be. I simply give you a feel, a sense of direction. Be aware and live through awareness.

I have heard. . . .

Mike told Pat he was going to a wake, and Pat offered to tag along. On the way Pat suggested a nip or two and they both got well sloshed. As a result Mike couldn't remember the address of the wake. "Where is your friend's house?" Pat asked.

"I forget the number, but I'm sure this is the street."

They had walked along for a few minutes when Mike squinted at a house that he thought was it. So they staggered in but the hall was dark. They opened the door and discovered a living room, which was also dark except for the faint glimmer of candles sitting on the piano. They went down in front of the piano, knelt and prayed. Pat stopped long enough to look at the piano. "Mike," he said, "I didn't know your friend, but he sure had a fine set of teeth."

This is the situation. This is how man is. The only thing that I would like to give to you is a taste of awareness. That will change your whole life. It is not a question of disciplining you, it is a question of making you luminous from within.

CHAPTER FIVE

The Healing Power
of Meditation

*T*he word "meditation" and the word "medicine" come from the same root. Medicine means that which heals the physical, and meditation means that which heals the spiritual. Both are healing powers.

Another thing to be remembered: the word "healing" and the word "whole" also come from the same root. To be healed simply means to be whole, not missing anything. Another connotation of the word—the word "holy" also comes from the same root. Healing, whole, holy, are not different in their root.

Meditation heals, makes you whole; and to be whole is to be holy. Holiness has nothing to do with belonging to any religion, belonging to any church. It simply means that inside you, you are entire, complete; nothing is missing, you are fulfilled. You are what existence wanted you to be. You have realized your potential.

OSHO ACTIVE MEDITATION TECHNIQUES*

Question: *"Your active meditations in the beginning tend to tighten muscles, causing pain everywhere. Is there any way to get over that?"*

*Please see *Meditation: The First and Last Freedom* for more details and instructions for Osho Active Meditations. Also available from St. Martin's Griffin.

Go on doing it! You will get over it—and the reasons are obvious. There are two reasons. First, it is a vigorous exercise and your body has to get attuned to it. So for three or four days you will feel that the whole body is aching. With any new exercise it will happen. But after four days you will get over it and your body will feel stronger than ever.

But this is not very basic. The basic thing goes deeper; it is what modern psychologists have come to know. Your body is not simply physical. In your body, in your muscles, in the structure of your body, many other things have entered through suppressions. If you suppress anger, the poison goes into the body. It goes into the muscles, it goes into the blood. If you suppress anything, it is not only a mental thing, it is also a physical one—because you are not really divided. You are not body and mind; you are "bodymind"—psychosomatic. You are both together. So whatever is done with your body reaches the mind and whatever is done with the mind reaches the body, as body and mind are two ends of the same entity.

For instance, if you get angry what happens to the body? Whenever you get angry certain poisons are released into the blood. Without those poisons you will not get mad enough to be angry. You have particular glands in the body, and those glands release certain chemicals. Now this is scientific; this is not just a philosophy. Your blood becomes poisoned.

That is why when you are angry you can do something that you cannot do ordinarily—because you are mad. You can push a big rock: you cannot do it ordinarily. You cannot even believe afterwards that you could have pushed this rock or thrown it or lifted it. When you are back to normal again, you will not be capable of lifting the rock again because you are not in the same state. Particular chemicals were circulating in the blood then; you were in an emergency condition; your total energy was brought to be active.

124 ■ BODY MIND BALANCING

When an animal gets angry, he gets angry. He has no morality about it, no teaching about it. He simply gets angry and the
anger is released. When you get angry, you get angry in a way
similar to the animal. But then there is society, morality, eti-
quette, and thousands of other things. You have to push the
anger down. You have to show that you are not angry; you have
to smile—a painted smile! You have to create a smile, and you
push the anger down. What is happening to the body? The body
was ready to fight—either to fight or to flee, to escape from the
danger, either to face it or escape from it. The body was ready
to do something: anger is just a readiness to do something. The
body was going to be violent, aggressive.

If you could be violent and aggressive, then the energy
would be released. But you cannot be—it is not convenient, so
you push it down. Then what will happen to all those muscles
that were ready to be aggressive? They will become crippled.
The energy pushes them to be aggressive, and you push them
backwards not to be aggressive. There will be conflict. In your
muscles, in your blood, in your body tissues, there will be conflict. They are ready to express something and you are pushing
them not to express it. You are suppressing them. Then your
body becomes crippled.

And this happens with every emotion. And this goes on day
after day for years. Then your body becomes crippled all over.
All the nerves become crippled as well. They are not flowing,
they are not liquid, they are not alive. They have become dead,
they have become poisoned. And they have all become entan-
gled. They are not natural.

Look at any animal and see the grace of his body. What happens to the human body? Why is it not so graceful? Why? Every
animal is so graceful: why is the human body not so graceful?
What has happened to it? You have done something with it: you

have crushed it and the natural spontaneity of its flow has gone. It has become stagnant. In every part of your body there is poison. In every muscle of your body there is suppressed anger, suppressed sexuality, suppressed greed—and everything—suppressed jealousy and hatred. Everything is suppressed there. Your body is really diseased.

Therefore, when you start doing these active meditations, all these poisons will be released. And wherever the body has become stagnant, it will have to melt, it will have to become liquid again. And this is a great effort. After forty years of living in a wrong way, then suddenly meditating, the whole body is in an upheaval. You will feel aching all over the body. But this aching is good, and you have to welcome it. Allow the body to become again a flow. Again it will become graceful and childlike; again you will gain the aliveness. But before that aliveness comes to you the dead parts have to be straightened, and this is going to be a little painful.

Psychologists say that we have created an armor around the body and that armor is the problem. If you are allowed total expression when you get angry, what will you do? When you get angry, you start crushing your teeth together; you want to do something with your nails and with your hands, because that's how your animal heritage will have it. You want to do something with your hands, to destroy something.

If you don't do anything your fingers will become crippled; they will lose their grace, the beauty. They will not be live limbs. And the poison is there. So when you shake hands with someone, really there is no touch, no life, because your hands are dead.

You can feel this. Touch a small child's hand—a subtle difference is there. When the child really gives you his hand . . . if he is not giving, then it is all right—he will withdraw. He will not give you a dead hand; he will simply withdraw. But if he wants to give you his hand, then you will feel as if it is melting into your hand. The warmth, the flow—as if the whole child has come to the hand. In his very touch, he expresses all the love that it is possible to express.

But the same child when grown up will shake hands as if his hand is just a dead instrument. He will not flow through it. This happens because of blocks. Anger is blocked. Before your hand becomes alive again to express love, it will have to pass through agony, it will have to pass through a deep expression of anger. If the anger is not released and it is blocking, love cannot come out of it.

Your whole body has become blocked, not only your hands. So you can embrace someone, you can take someone near your chest, but that is not synonymous with taking someone near your heart. They are two different things. You can take someone near your chest: this is a physical phenomenon. But if you have armor around your heart, a blocking of emotions, then the person remains as distant as he ever was; no intimacy is possible. But if you really take a person near, and there is no armor, no wall between you and the person, then the heart will melt into the other. There will be a meeting, a communion.

Your body has to release many poisons. You have become toxic, and you will have pain because those poisons have settled in. Now I am creating chaos again. This meditation is to create chaos within you so that you can be rearranged, so that a new arrangement becomes possible. You must be destroyed as you are, only then can the new be born. There will be pain, but this pain is worthwhile.

So go on doing the meditation and allow the body to have pain. Allow the body not to resist; allow the body to move into this agony. This agony comes from your past, but it will go. If you are ready, it will go. And when it goes, then for the first time you will have a body. Right now you have only an imprisonment, a capsule; you are in essence dead. You are encapsulated; you do not have an agile, alive body. Even animals have more beautiful, more alive bodies than you.

By the way, that is why we have become so much obsessed with clothes—because the body is not worth showing. Whenever you stand naked, you will see what you have done to your body. Clothes go on hiding your body from you.

This disease results in a vicious cycle because if you do not have an alive body, you want to hide it, and when you hide it, it becomes more and more dead—because then there is no need to be alert about its being alive.

Through centuries of clothing we have lost touch with our own bodies. If your head is cut off and you encounter your own body without a head, I am sure you will not be able to recognize that this is your body—or will you be able to recognize it? No, you will not be able to recognize it because you are not even acquainted with your own body. You do not have any feeling about it; you are simply living in it without caring about it.

We have done much violence to our bodies. So in this chaotic meditation I am forcing your bodies to be alive again. Many blocks will be broken; many settled things will become unsettled again; many systems will become liquid again. There will be pain, but welcome it. It is a blessing and you will overcome it. Continue! There is no need to think what to do. You simply continue the meditation. I have seen thousands and thousands of people passing through the same process. Within a few days the pain is gone. And when the pain is gone, you will feel a subtle joy around your body.

You cannot have it right now because the pain is there. You

may know it or you may not know it but the pain is there all over your body. You have simply become unconscious about it because it has always been with you. Whatever is always there, you become unconscious about. Through meditation you will become conscious and then the mind will say, "Don't do this; the whole body is aching." Do not listen to the mind. Simply go on doing the meditation.

Within a certain period the pain will be expelled. And when it has, when your body has again become receptive and there is no block, no poisons around it, you will always have a subtle feeling of joy wrapped around you. Whatever you are doing or not doing, you will always feel a subtle vibration of joy around your body.

Really, joy only means that your body is in a symphony, nothing else—that your body is in a musical rhythm, nothing else. Joy is not pleasure; pleasure has to be derived from something else. Joy is just to be yourself—alive, fully vibrant, vital; a feeling of a subtle music around your body, and within your body a symphony—that is joy. You can be joyful when your body is flowing, when it is a riverlike flow.

It will come but first you will have to pass through suffering, through pain. That is part of your destiny because you have created it. But it will go. If you do not stop in the middle, it will go. If you stop in the middle, then the old settlement will be there again. Within four or five days you will feel okay—just the old, as you have always been. Be aware of that state of being okay.

THE STATE OF LET-GO

It is difficult to be in a state of let-go because it has been always condemned as laziness. It is not acceptable in a workaholic society. Let-go means you start living in a saner way. You are no longer madly seeking money, you don't go on working continuously; you work just for your material needs. But there are spiritual needs too!

Work is a necessity to earn material needs. Let-go is necessary for spiritual needs. But the majority of humanity has been completely boycotted from any spiritual growth.

Let-go is one of the most beautiful spaces. You simply exist, doing nothing, sitting silently, and the grass grows by itself. You simply enjoy the songs of the birds, the greenness of the trees, the multidimensional, psychedelic colors of the flowers. You don't have to do anything to experience existence; you have to stop doing. You have to be in an absolutely unoccupied state, with no tensions, with no worries.

In this state of tranquility you come into a certain tuning with the music that surrounds us. You suddenly become aware of the beauty of the sun. There are millions of people who have never enjoyed a sunset, who have never enjoyed a sunrise. They cannot afford to. They are continuously working and producing—not for themselves, but for the cunning vested interests: those who are in power, those who are capable of manipulating human beings.

Naturally they teach you that work is something great—it is in their interest. And the conditioning has become so deep that even you don't know why you cannot relax.

Even on holidays people go on doing something or other. They cannot enjoy a holiday, just relaxing on the beach and enjoying the ocean and the fresh and salty air. No, they will do any stupid thing. If they have nothing to do, they may just take their refrigerator apart—which had been functioning perfectly well— or they may destroy an old grandfather clock, which had been functioning for centuries; they are trying to improve upon it. But basically they cannot sit silently; that is the problem. They have to do something; they have to go somewhere.

On every holiday people are rushing toward health resorts, beaches, not to rest there—they don't have time to rest, because millions of people are going there. Holidays are the best time to remain at home, because the whole city has gone to the beach. Bumper to bumper, cars are going . . . and by the time they reach the beach it is full of people; they cannot find even a small place to lie down. I have seen pictures of such beaches. Even the ocean must be laughing at the stupidity of these people.

For a few minutes they will lie down, and then they need ice cream and they need Coca-Cola. And they have brought their portable television sets and everybody is listening to those or their transistor radios. And then the time is over, and there is the marathon race back toward home.

On holidays more accidents happen in the world than on any other days: more people are killed, more cars are crashed. It is strange! And for the earlier five days in the week—the working days—people are hoping, waiting with great longing for the holiday to come. And in those two weekend days, they simply wait for their offices and factories to open again.

People have completely forgotten the language of relaxation. They have been made to forget it.

Every child is born with an inner capacity; you don't have to teach the child how to relax. Just watch a child—he is relaxed, he is in a let-go. But you won't allow him to enjoy this state of paradise. You will soon civilize him.

Every child is primitive, uncivilized, and the parents and the teachers and everybody else are after the children to civilize them, to make them part of the society. No one seems to care that society is absolutely insane. It would be good if the child could remain as he is and not be initiated into society and the so-called civilization.

But with all good wishes the parents cannot leave the child alone. They have to teach him to work, they have to teach him to be productive, they have to teach him to be competitive. They have to teach him that "Unless you are at the top you have failed us."

Thus everyone is running to be at the top.

How can you relax?

I heard a story about when the railway lines were first laid down in India:

> The British engineer who was overseeing the work that was going on was amazed to see that every day a young Indian, a villager, would come and lie down under the shade of a big tree and watch the workers working and the engineers instructing them. The engineer became interested: every day this strange fellow comes. He brings his food with him, he takes his lunch and rests, then sleeps in the afternoon under the shade of the tree.
>
> Finally the engineer could not resist the temptation and he asked the villager, "Why don't you start working? You come anyway every day, and you waste your time just lying down watching."
>
> The villager asked, "Working? But for what?"
>
> The engineer said, "You will earn money!"
>
> The villager asked, "But what will I do with the money?"
>
> The engineer said, "You stupid man, you don't know what can be done with the money? When you have money you can relax and enjoy!"
>
> The poor villager said, "This is strange, because I am already relaxed and enjoying! This is going about it in such a roundabout way: working hard, earning money, and then enjoying and relaxing. But I am doing that already!"

*   *   *

Children come with the intrinsic, intuitive quality of let-go. They are utterly relaxed. That's why all children are beautiful. Have you ever thought about it? All children, without exception, have a tremendous grace, aliveness, and beauty. And these children are going to grow up, and all their beauty and their grace will disappear.

It is very difficult to find a grown-up man with the same grace, with the same beauty, with the same aliveness. If you can find a man with childlike innocence and relaxation, you have found a sage.

That's how we have defined the sage in the East: he attains his childhood again. After experiencing all the ups and downs in life, finally he decides, out of experience—the decision comes by itself—that what he was in his childhood he has to be again before death comes.

I teach you let-go, because that's the only thing that can make you a sage. No church will help, no theology, no religion, because none of them teach you let-go. They all insist on work, on the dignity of labor. They use beautiful words to enslave you, to exploit you. They are in conspiracy with the parasites of society.

I am not against work; work has its own utility—but only utility. It cannot become your life's all and all. It is an absolute necessity that you have food, that you have clothes, that you have shelter. Work, but don't become addicted to work. The moment you are out of work, you should know how to relax. And it does not take much wisdom to relax; it is a simple art. It is so simple because you already knew how to do it when you were born; you just have to be awaken it from its dormant state. It has to be provoked.

All methods of meditation are nothing but ways to help you to remember the art of let-go. I say remember, because you once knew it. And you know it still, but that knowledge is being repressed by society.

Simple principles have to be remembered: The body should be the starting point. Lie down on your bed—you do this every day, so nothing special is necessary—and before sleep comes, with closed eyes start watching the energy from your feet. Move from there—just watch inside: Is there some tension somewhere? in the legs, in the thighs, in the stomach? Is there some strain? And if you find some tension somewhere, simply try to relax it. And don't move from that point unless you feel relaxation has come.

Go through the hands—because your hands are your mind; they are connected with your mind. If your right hand is tense, the left side of your brain will be tense. If your left hand is tense, the right side of your brain will be tense. So first go through the hands—they are almost the branches of your mind—and then reach finally to the mind.

When the whole body is relaxed, the mind is already 90 percent relaxed, because the body is nothing but an extension of the mind. Then simply watch the 10 percent tension that is in your mind, and just by watching the clouds will disappear. It will take you a few days; you have to acquire the knack. And it will revive your childhood experience, when you were so relaxed.

Have you ever noticed that children go on falling every day, but they don't get hurt, rarely get fractures. You try it. Pick a child and whenever the child falls, you also fall.

A psychoanalyst tried an experiment. He announced in the newspapers, "I will pay good money if somebody will come to my house and just follow my child for the whole day. Whatever my child does, you have to do it too."

A young wrestler turned up and said, "I am ready; where is the child?"

But by the middle of the day the wrestler was flat on his back. He had already sustained two fractures, because he did everything that the child had done. And the child got very excited. This is strange, he thought. So he would jump unnecessarily, and then the wrestler would jump; he would climb a tree, and then the wrestler would climb it; and he would jump from the tree, and the wrestler would follow. And this continued. The child completely forgot about food, about anything, because he was enjoying the misery of the wrestler so much.

By the afternoon the wrestler simply refused to go on. He said to the psychoanalyst, "Keep your money. This child of yours will kill me by the end of the day. I am already ready to go to the hospital. This child is dangerous. Don't do this experiment with anybody else."

Every child has so much energy, and still he is not tense. Have you watched a child sleeping? Have you watched a child just sucking his own thumb, enjoying it, dreaming beautiful dreams? His whole body is in a deep let-go.

It happens—it is a known fact—that every day around the world drunkards fall but they don't get fractures. Every morning they are found in some gutter and brought home. But it is a strange fact that they go on falling. The drunkard will not get hurt, because he does not know he is falling, so he does not become tense. He simply falls without becoming tense. It is the tenseness that gives you fractures. If you can fall relaxed, you will not be hurt. Drunkards know it, children know it; how did you manage to forget?

Start from your bed, every night, and within a few days you will have acquired the knack. Once you know the secret—nobody can teach it to you, you will have to search within your own body—then any time during the day you will be able relax. And to be a master of relaxation is one of the most beautiful experiences in the world. It is the beginning of a great journey toward spirituality, because when you are completely in a let-go, you are no longer a body.

Have you ever observed the simple fact that you become aware of your body only when there is some tension, some strain, some pain? Have you ever become aware of your head without a headache?

If your whole body is relaxed, you simply forget that you are a body. And in that forgetfulness of the body is the remembering of a new phenomenon that is hidden inside the body: your spiritual being.

Let-go is the way to know that you are not the body, but something eternal, immortal.

There is no need for any other religion in the world. Just the simple art of let-go will turn every human being into a religious person. Religion is not believing in God, religion is not believing in the pope, religion is not believing in any ideological system. Religion is knowing that which is eternal within you: that which is the truth of your existence, that which is your divinity, and that which is your beauty, your grace, your splendor.

The art of let-go is synonymous with experiencing the immaterial, the immeasurable: your authentic being.

There are a few moments when, without being aware, you are in a let-go. For example, when you are really laughing—belly laughing, not just from the head, but from your belly—you are relaxed without your knowing, you are in a let-go. That's why laughter is so health-giving. There is no other medicine that can help you more in attaining well-being.

But laughter has been stopped by the same conspirators who have stopped your awareness of let-go. The whole of humanity has been turned into a serious, psychologically sick mess.

Have you heard the giggle of a small child? His whole body

participates in it. And when you laugh, it is very rare that your whole body laughs—it is usually just an intellectual, heady thing.

My own understanding is that laughter is far more important than any prayer, because prayer will not relax you. On the contrary, it may make you more tense. In laughter you suddenly forget all the conditioning, all the training, all seriousness. Suddenly you are out of it, just for a moment. Next time you laugh, be alert about how relaxed you are. And find other times when you are relaxed.

After making love you are relaxed . . . although the same company of conspirators does not allow you to be relaxed even after making love. The man simply turns to the other side and pretends to go to sleep, but deep down he is feeling guilty that he has committed a sin again. The woman is crying, because she feels she has been used.

There cannot be a greater conspiracy against humanity. The man wants to finish the whole thing as quickly as possible. Inside him he is carrying the Bible, the Koran, Shrimad Bhagavadgita, and they all speak against what he is doing. He is also convinced that he is doing something wrong. So naturally, the quicker it is over the better. And afterwards he feels very bad. How can he relax? He becomes more tense. And because he is so quick, the woman never reaches her peak. By the time she starts, he is finished. Naturally, the woman starts believing that man is something more like an animal.

In the churches and the temples, you will find only women, old women particularly. And when the priest talks about sin, they know! It was absolutely sin, because they had gained no pleasure from it; they were used like a commodity—sexual objects.

On the other hand, if you are free of guilt, free of all inhibitions, love will give you a tremendous experience of let-go.

You have to look into your life to find some natural experience of let-go. Swimming can provide such a moment. If you are a real swimmer you can manage just to float, not to swim, and then you will find tremendous let-go—just going with the river, not making any movement against the current, becoming part of the current.

You have to gather experiences of let-go from different sources, and soon you will have the whole secret in your hands. It will free you from the workaholic conditioning.

It does not mean that you will become lazy; on the contrary, the more relaxed you are, the more powerful you are, the more energy gathers when you are relaxed. Your work will start having a quality of creativity—not productivity. Whatever you do, you will do with such totality, with such love. And you will have tremendous energy to do it. So understand that let-go is not against work. In fact, let-go transforms work into a creative experience.

Let me tell you a few jokes so you can enjoy total laughter. It takes away all tensions from your face, from your body, from your stomach, and suddenly you feel a totally different kind of energy within you; otherwise most people always feel they have knots in their stomachs.

> Paddy's friend, Joe, was taking a night course in adult education. "Who is Ronald Reagan?" he asked Paddy.
>
> "I don't know," Paddy replied.
>
> "He is the president of the United States," said Joe. "Now, do you know who Margaret Thatcher is?"
>
> "No," said Paddy.
>
> "She is the prime minister of Britain," said Joe. "You see, you should go to night school like I do."
>
> "Now I have a question for you," said Paddy. "Do you know who Mick O'Sullivan is?"
>
> "I don't," admitted Joe.

"Well," said Paddy, "he is the guy who is screwing your wife while you are at night school."

Jesus and Moses are out one Sunday afternoon for a round of golf. Moses drives first and the ball goes straight down the fairway. Jesus gets ready and on his first drive slices the ball into some tall grass.

"Holy Moses!" cries Jesus. But Moses, being a good fellow, offers Jesus the chance to place his ball on the fairway with no penalty. But Jesus is stubborn and turns down the offer. Moses then says, "Come on, Jesus, you can't take a shot in such tall grass."

"If Arnold Palmer can do it," replies Jesus "so can I." Jesus then takes a smash and knocks the ball, *splash!* into a pond. Then Moses hits his second shot straight onto the green and returns to watch Jesus. Jesus is rolling up his jeans.

"Jesus, please!" cries Moses, "I implore you to just place your ball on the fairway. It will take a miracle to make such a shot!"

"If Arnold Palmer can do it," replies Jesus, "so can I," and he strides off across the top of the water. A gardener, who has been watching the scene, approaches Moses and says, "Just who does that guy think he is, Jesus Christ?"

"No such luck," replies Moses. "He thinks he is Arnold Palmer!"

EVERYDAY MEDITATION

Whenever you find time, for a few minutes just relax the breathing system, nothing else—there is no need to relax the whole body. Sitting in the train or plane, or in the car, nobody will become aware that you are doing something. Just relax the breathing system. Let it be as when it is functioning naturally. Then close your eyes and watch the breathing going in, coming out, going in . . .

Do not concentrate. If you concentrate, you create trouble, because then everything becomes a disturbance. If you try to concentrate sitting in the car, then the noise of the car becomes a disturbance, the person sitting beside you becomes a disturbance.

Meditation is not concentration. It is simple awareness. You simply relax and watch the breathing. In that watching, nothing is excluded. The car is humming—perfectly okay, accept it. The traffic is passing—that's okay, part of life. Your fellow passenger is snoring by your side—just accept it. Nothing is rejected. You are not to narrow down your consciousness.

Concentration is a narrowing down of your consciousness so you become one-pointed, but everything else becomes a competition. You are fighting everything else because you are afraid that the point may be lost. You may be distracted, and that becomes disturbing. Then you need seclusion, the Himalayas. You need India, and a room where you can sit silently, nobody disturbing you at all.

No, that is not right—that cannot become a life process. It is isolating yourself. It does have some good results—you will feel more tranquil, more calm—but those results are temporary. That's why you feel again and again that tone is lost. Once you don't have the conditions in which it can happen, it is lost.

A meditation in which you need certain prerequisites, in which certain conditions need to be fulfilled, is not meditation at all—because you will not be able to do it when you are dying. Death will be such a distraction. If life distracts you, just think about death. You will not be able to die meditatively, and then the whole thing is futile, lost. You will die again tense, anxious, in misery, in suffering, and you create immediately your next birth of the same type.

Let death be the criterion. Anything that can be done even while you are dying is real—and that can be done anywhere; anywhere, and with no condition as a necessity. If sometimes the conditions are good, then fine, enjoy them. If not, it makes no difference. Do it even in the marketplace.

Do not make any attempt to control it, because all control is from the mind, so meditation can never be a controlled thing.

Mind cannot meditate. Meditation is something beyond the mind, or below the mind, but never within the mind. So if the mind remains watching and controlling, it is not meditation; it is concentration. Concentration is a mind effort. It brings the qualities of the mind to their peak. A scientist concentrates, a soldier concentrates; a hunter, a research worker, a mathematician, they all concentrate. These are mind activities.

You can choose any time. There is no need to make a fixed time. Use whatever time is available. In the bathroom when you have ten minutes, just sit under the shower and meditate. In the morning, in the afternoon, just four or five times, for small intervals, meditate, and you will see that it becomes a constant nourishment. There is no need to do it for twenty-four hours.

Just a cup of meditation will do. No need to drink the whole river. Just a cup of tea will do. And make it as easy as possible. Easy is right. Make it as natural as possible. And don't run after it—just do it whenever you find time. Don't make a habit of it, because all habits are of the mind, and a real person in fact has no habits.

RELAXED AND EASY

For relaxation one has to be very comfortable, so make yourself comfortable. Whatever posture you want to take in the chair, take. Close your eyes and relax your body. Just from the toes up to the head, feel inside where you feel the tension. If you feel it at the knee, relax the knee. Just touch the knee and say to the knee, "Please relax." If you feel some tension in the shoulders, just touch the place and say, "Please relax."

Relax in your chair, have the light as dark or dim as you like, but the light should not be bright. Tell everybody for these twenty minutes you are not to be disturbed, no phone calls, nothing whatsoever, as if the outside world does not exist for those twenty minutes. Close the doors, relax in your chair with loose clothes so there is no tightness anywhere, and start feeling where the tension is. You will find many spots of tension. Those have to be relaxed first, because if the body is not relaxed, the mind cannot be either. The body creates the situation for the mind to relax. The body becomes the vehicle of relaxation.

Wherever you feel some tension, touch your body with deep love, with compassion. The body is your servant, and you have not paid anything for it—it is simply a gift. And the body is so complicated, so tremendously complex that science has not been able yet to make anything like a body. But we never think about that; we don't love the body. On the contrary; we feel angry about it.

The so-called saints have taught many foolish things to people—that the body is the enemy, that the body is your degradation, that the body is pulling you downwards, that the body is the sin; it is all sin. If you want to commit a sin, the body helps, that's true. But the responsibility is yours, not the body's. If you want to meditate, the body is ready to help you do that too. If you want to go downwards, the body follows you. If you want to go upwards, the body follows you. The body is not the culprit at all. The whole responsibility belongs to your own consciousness— but we always try to find scapegoats. The body has been one of the most ancient scapegoats. You can throw anything, and the body is dumb. It cannot retaliate, it cannot answer, it cannot say that you are wrong so whatever you say, the body has no reaction against it.

So go on all over the body and surround it with loving compassion, with deep sympathy, with care. This will take at least five minutes, and you will start feeling very very limp, relaxed, almost sleepy. Then bring your consciousness to the breathing: relax the breathing.

The body is our outermost part, the consciousness the innermost, and the breathing is the bridge that joins them together. That's why once breathing disappears, the person is dead— because the bridge is broken; now the body cannot function as your home, your abode.

So when the body is relaxed, just close your eyes and see your breathing; relax that too. Have a little talk to your breathing: "Please relax. Be natural." You will see that the moment you say, "Please relax," there will be a subtle click. Ordinarily breathing has become very unnatural, and we have forgotten how to relax it because we are so continuously tense that it has become almost habitual for the breathing to remain tense. So just tell it to relax two or three times and then just remain silent.

CHAPTER SIX

The Door to Consciousness

*M*illions *of people are living according to the mirror. They think that what they see in the mirror is their face. They think this is their name, this is their identity, and that is all.*

You will have to go a little deeper. You will have to close your eyes. You will have to watch within. You will have to become silent. Unless you come to a point of absolute silence inside, you will never know who you are. I cannot tell it to you. There is no way of telling it. Everybody has to find it.

But you are—that much is certain. The only question is to reach to your innermost core, to find yourself. And that's what I have been teaching all these years. What I call meditation is nothing but a device to find yourself.

Don't ask me. Don't ask anybody. You have the answer within you, and you have to go deep down into yourself to discover it. And it is so close—just a hundred-and-eighty-degree turn and you will be facing it.

And you will be surprised that you are not your name, you are not your face, your body, you are not even your mind.

You are part of this whole existence, of all its beauty, grandeur, blissfulness, its tremendous ecstasy.

Knowing oneself is all that consciousness means.

CENTER AND CIRCUMFERENCE

The body in itself is nothing. It is luminous because of something that is beyond the body. The glory of the body is not in the body itself—it is a host—the glory is because of the guest. If you forget the guest, then it is sheer indulgence. If you remember the guest, then loving the body, celebrating the body is part of worship.

The modern worship of the body is meaningless. Hence, people go after health food, massage, Rolfing, and in a thousand and one ways they somehow try to create meaning in their lives. But look into their eyes; a great emptiness exists. You can see they have missed the target. The fragrance is not there, the flower has not flowered. Deep inside, they are just desert-like, lost, not knowing what to do. They go on doing many things for the body, but they are missing the target.

Here is an anecdote I have heard:

Rosenfeld walked into the house with a grin on his face. "You will never guess what a bargain I just got," he told his wife. "I bought four polyester, steel-belted, radial, wide-tread, white-walled, heavy-duty tires, on sale yet!"

"Are you nuts?" said Mrs. Rosenfeld. "What did you buy tires for? You don't even have a car."

"So," said Rosenfeld, "you buy brassieres, don't you?"

If the center is missing, then you can go on decorating the periphery. It may deceive others, but it cannot fulfill you. It may even deceive you sometimes, because even one's own lie repeated too many times starts appearing like a truth, but it cannot fulfill you, and it cannot give contentment. People try hard to enjoy life, but there seems to be no rejoicing. Remember that whenever you are trying to enjoy, you will miss. When you are trying to achieve happiness, you will miss. The very effort to achieve happiness is absurd—because happiness is here: you cannot achieve it. Nothing has to be done about it; you have simply to allow it. It is happening, it is all around you; within, without, only happiness is. Nothing else is real. Watch, look deep into the world, into trees, birds, rocks, rivers, into the stars, moon and sun, into people, animals—look deep: existence is made out of the stuff of happiness, joy. It is made of bliss. Nothing need be done about it. Your very doing may be the barrier. Relax and it fulfills you; relax and it rushes into you; relax and it overflows you.

People are tense. Tension arises when you are chasing something; relaxation arises when you are allowing something.

People are chasing, chasing hard, trying to get something out of life, trying to squeeze life. Nothing comes of it because that is not the way. You cannot squeeze life; you have to surrender to it. You cannot conquer life. You have to be so courageous to be defeated by life. Defeat is victory there, and the effort to be victorious is going to prove to be nothing but your final, utter failure.

Life cannot be conquered because the part cannot conquer the whole. It is as if a small drop of water is trying to conquer the ocean. Yes, the small drop can fall into the ocean and become the ocean, but it cannot conquer the ocean. In fact, dropping into the ocean, slipping into the ocean is the way to conquer.

People are trying to find happiness, hence the overconcern with the body. It is almost an obsession. It has gone beyond the limits of concern to obsession with the body. They are making an effort to have some contact with happiness through the body, and that is not possible.

The second problem is that the mind is competitive. You may

not be really in love with body, you may be just competing with others. Because others are doing things, you have to do them. And the American mind is the most shallow, ambitious mind that has ever existed. It is a very worldly mind. That's why the businessman has become the top-most reality in America. Everything else has faded into the background; the businessman, the man who controls money, is the top-most reality. In India, brahmins were the top-most reality—the seekers of God. In Europe, the aristocrats were the top-most reality—cultured, educated, alert, in tune with the subtle nuances of life: music, art, poetry, sculpture, architecture, classical dances, languages—Greek and Latin. Under Communism the proletariat, the downtrodden, the oppressed, the laborer is the top-most reality. Under capitalism it is the businessman, the one who controls money.

Money is the most competitive realm. You need not have culture, you need only have money. You need not know anything about music or poetry. You need not know anything about ancient literature, history, religion, philosophy—no, you need not know. If you have a big bank balance, you are important. That's why I say the American mind is the most shallow mind that has ever existed. It has turned everything into commerce. It is continuously in competition. Even if you purchase a Van Gogh or a Picasso, you don't purchase because it is a Picasso. You purchase it because the neighbors have purchased one. They have one in their drawing room, so how can you afford not to have one? You have to have it. You may not know even how to hang it properly since it is difficult to know, with a Picasso, whether it is hanging upside down or right side up. You may not even know whether it is an authentic Picasso. You may not look at it much but you have acquired it because others have. You simply flaunt your money and possessions because whatever is costly is thought to be significant.

Money and the neighbors seem to be the only criterion in deciding American success. You have to keep up with the Joneses. If they have saunas in their bathrooms, everyone has to have one to be part of the "in" crowd. Otherwise you look poor. If everyone has a house in the hills, you have to have one too. You may not know how to enjoy the hills or you simply may be bored there. Or you may take your TV and radio there and just listen to the same programs you were listening to in your old home. What difference does it make where you live? The answer is that it matters because it matters to others. And so on it goes.

I have heard.

Old Luke and his wife were known as the stingiest couple in the valley. Luke died and a few months later his wife lay dying. She called in a neighbor and said weakly, "Ruthie, bury me in my black silk dress, but before you do, cut the back out and make a new dress out of it. It is good material and I hate to waste it."

"Could not do that," said Ruthie. "When you and Luke walk up them golden stairs, what would them angels say if your dress ain't got a back in it?"

"They won't be looking at me," she said. "I buried Luke without his pants."

The concern is always the other—Luke will be without pants so everybody will be looking at him. The American concern is always with the other.

Have you watched a child just running, shouting, dancing for nothing at all—because he has nothing? If you ask him, "Why are you so happy?" he will not be able to answer you. He will really think that you are mad. Is there any need to have a reason to be happy? The child will simply be shocked that "why" is asked. He will shrug his shoulders and go on his way and start singing and dancing again. The child has nothing. He is not a prime minister yet, he is not a president of the United States, he is not a Rockefeller. He owns nothing—maybe a few shells or a few stones that he has collected on the seashore, that's all.

An American's life ends when life ends. When the body ends, the American ends. Hence, the American is very afraid of death. Because of his fear of death, the American goes on trying to prolong his life in any way, sometimes to absurd lengths. Now there are many Americans who are just vegetating in hospitals or in mental asylums. They are not living; they are long since dead. They are just kept alive by the physicians, medicines, and modern equipment. Somehow they just hang on.

The fear of death is so tremendous—once gone you are gone forever and nothing will survive—because the American knows only the body and nothing else. If you know only the body you are going to be very poor. First, you will always be afraid of death, and one who is afraid to die will be afraid to live— because life and death are so intertwined that if you are afraid to die you will become afraid to live. It is life that brings death, so if you are afraid of death, how can you really love life? The fear will be there. It is life that brings death; you cannot live it totally. If death ends everything, if that is your belief and understanding, then your life will be a life of rushing and chasing, because death is always coming and you cannot be patient. Hence you understand the American mania for speed: everything has to be done fast because death is approaching; try to manage as many things as possible before you die. Try to stuff your being with as many experiences as possible before you die, because once you are dead, you are dead.

This creates a great meaninglessness and, of course, anguish and anxiety. If nothing is going to survive the body, then whatever you do cannot be very deep. Then whatever you do cannot satisfy you. If death is the end and nothing survives, then life cannot have any meaning and significance. Then it is a tale told by an idiot, full of fury and noise, signifying nothing.

The Baul/conscious man knows that he is in the body, but he is not the body. He loves the body; it is his abode, his house, his home. He is not against the body because it is foolish to be against your own home, but he is not a materialist. He is earthly but not a materialist. He is very realistic, but not a materialist. He knows that in dying nothing dies. Death comes but life continues.

I have heard:

The funeral service was over and Desmond, the undertaker, found himself standing beside an elderly gent.

"One of the relatives?" asked the mortician.

"Yes, I am," answered the senior citizen.

"How old are you?"

"Ninety-four."

"Hmm," said Desmond, "hardly pays you to make the trip home."

The whole idea is of bodily life: if you are ninety-four, finished! Then it hardly pays to go back home; then better to die. What is the point of going back? You will have to come back again. It hardly pays . . . if death is the only reality, then whether you are ninety-four or twenty-four, how much difference does it make? Then the difference is of only a few years. Then the very young start feeling old, and the child starts feeling already dead. Once you understand that this body is the only life, then what is the point of it all? Then why carry it on?

Camus has written that the only basic metaphysical problem

for man is suicide. I agree with him. If body is the only reality and there is nothing within you that is beyond body, then of course that is the most important thing to consider, brood, and meditate on. Why not commit suicide? Why wait until ninety-four? And why suffer all sorts of problems and miseries on the way? If one is going to die, then why not die today? Why get up again tomorrow morning? It seems futile.

On the one hand the American is constantly running from one place to another to somehow grab the experience, somehow not to miss the experience. He is running all around the world, from one town to another, from one country to another, from one hotel to another. He is running from one guru to another, from one church to another, searching, because death is coming. On the one hand is a constant, mad chasing, and on the other hand is a deep-down apprehension that everything is useless—because death will end all. So whether you lived a rich life or you lived a poor life, whether you were intelligent or unintelligent, whether you were a great lover or missed, what difference does it make? Finally death comes, and it equalizes everybody: the wise and the foolish, the sages and the sinners, the enlightened and the stupid, all go down into the earth and disappear. So what is the point of it all? Whether it be a Buddha or a Jesus or a Judas; what difference does it make? Jesus dies on the cross, Judas commits suicide the next day—both disappear into the earth.

On the other hand, there is a fear that you may miss and others may attain; there is a deep apprehension that even if you get, nothing is got; even if you arrive, you arrive nowhere because death comes and destroys everything.

The conscious man lives in the body, loves his body, celebrates it, but he is not the body. He knows that there is something in him that will survive all deaths. He knows that there is something in him that is eternal and time cannot destroy it. This he has come to feel through meditation, love, prayer. This he has come to feel inside his own being. He is unafraid. He is unafraid of death because he knows what life is. And he is not chasing happiness, because he knows God is sending him millions of opportunities; he has just to allow.

Can't you see the trees are rooted in the ground? They cannot go anywhere, and still they are happy. They cannot chase happiness, certainly; they cannot go and seek happiness. They are rooted in the ground, they cannot move, but can't you see the happiness? Can't you see their joy when it is raining, their great contentment when winds are running hither and thither? Can't you feel their dance? They are rooted; they go nowhere. Still, life comes to them.

All comes—you just create the capacity; all comes—you just allow it. Life is ready to happen to you. You are creating so many barriers, and the greatest barrier that you can create is chasing. Because of your chasing and running, whenever life comes and knocks at your door she never finds you there. You are always somewhere else. You go on chasing life and life goes on chasing you, and the meeting never happens.

Be . . . just be, and wait, and be patient.

THE HARMONY OF BODY, MIND, AND SOUL

Your body is energy, your mind is energy, your soul is energy. Then what is the difference among these three? The difference is only of a different rhythm, different wavelengths, that's all. The body is gross—energy functioning in a gross way, in a visible way.

Mind is a little more subtle, but still not too subtle, because you can close your eyes and you can see the thoughts moving; they can be seen. They are not as visible as your body; your body is visible to everybody else, it is publicly visible. Your thoughts are privately visible. Nobody else can see your thoughts; only you can see them—or people who have worked very deeply into seeing thoughts. But ordinarily they are not visible to others.

And the third, the ultimate layer inside you, is that of consciousness. It is not even visible to you. It cannot be reduced into an object; it remains subject.

If all these three energies function in harmony, you are healthy and whole. If these energies don't function in harmony and accord, you are ill, unhealthy; you are no more whole. And to be whole is to be holy.

My effort is to help you so that your body, your mind, your consciousness can all dance in one rhythm, in a togetherness, in a deep harmony—not in conflict at all, but in cooperation.

Consciousness is energy, purest energy; mind is not so pure; body is still less pure. Body is much too mixed, and mind is also not totally pure. Consciousness is total pure energy. But you can know this consciousness only if you make a cosmos out of the three, and not a chaos. People are living in chaos: their bodies say one thing, their bodies want to go in one direction; their minds are completely oblivious of the body—because for centuries you have been taught that you are not the body, for centuries you have been told that the body is your enemy, that you have to fight with it, that you have to destroy it, that the body is sin.

Because of all these ideas—silly and stupid as they are, harmful and poisonous as they are, but they have been taught for so long that they have become part of your collective mind, they are there—you don't experience your body in a rhythmic dance with yourself.

Hence my insistence on dancing and music, because it is only in dance that you will feel that your body, your mind, and you are functioning together. And the joy is infinite when all these function together; the richness is great.

Consciousness is the highest form of energy. And when all these three energies function together, the fourth arrives. The fourth is always present when these three function together. When these three function in an organic unity, the fourth is always there; the fourth is nothing but that organic unity.

In the East, we have called that fourth simply "the fourth"— turiya; we have not given it any name. The three have names, the fourth is nameless. To know the fourth is to know God. Let us say it in this way: God is when you are an organic orgasmic unity. God is not when you are a chaos, a disunity, a conflict. When you are a house divided against yourself there is no God.

When you are tremendously happy with yourself, happy as you are, blissful as you are, grateful as you are, and all your energies are dancing together, when you are an orchestra of all your energies, God is. That feeling of total unity is what God is. God is not a person somewhere, God is the experience of the three falling in such unity that the fourth arises. And the fourth is more than the sum total of the parts.

If you dissect a painting, you will find the canvas and the colors, but the painting is not simply the sum total of the canvas and the colors; it is something more. That "something more" is expressed through the painting, color, canvas, the artist, but that "something more" is the beauty. Dissect the rose flower, and you will find all the chemicals and things it is constituted of, but the beauty will disappear. It was not just the sum total of the parts; it was more.

The whole is more than the sum total of the parts; it expresses through the parts, but it is more. To understand that it is more is to understand God. God is that more, that plus. It is not a question of theology; it cannot be decided by logical argumentation. You have to feel beauty, you have to feel music, you have to feel dance. And ultimately you have to feel the dance in your body, mind, and soul.

You have to learn how to play on these three energies so that they all become an orchestra. Then God is—not that you see God, there is nothing to be seen; God is the ultimate seer, it is witnessing. Learn to melt your body, mind, soul; find out ways when you can function as a unity.

It happens many times with runners . . . You will not think of running as a meditation, but runners sometimes have felt a tremendous experience of meditation. They were surprised, because they were not looking for it—who thinks that a runner is going to experience God?—but it has happened, and now running is becoming more and more a new kind of meditation. It can happen in running. If you have ever been a runner, if you have enjoyed running in the early morning when the air is fresh and young and the whole world is coming out of sleep, awakening, and you were running and your body was functioning beautifully, and the fresh air, and the new world again born out of the darkness of the night, and everything singing all around, and you were feeling so alive . . . A moment comes when the runner disappears, and there is only running. The body, mind, and soul start functioning together; suddenly an inner orgasm is released.

Runners have sometimes come accidentally on the experience of the fourth, turiya, although they will miss it because they will think it was just because of running that they enjoyed the moment; that it was a beautiful day, that the body was healthy and the world was beautiful, and it was just a certain mood. They will not take note of it. But if they take note of it, my own observation is that a runner can more easily come close to meditation than anybody else. Jogging can be of immense help;

swimming can be of immense help. All these things have to be transformed into meditations.

Drop the old ideas about meditations, that just sitting underneath a tree with a yoga posture is meditation. That is only one of the ways, and it may be suitable for a few people but is not suitable for all. For a small child it is not meditation, it is torture. For a young man who is alive and vibrant, it is repression, not meditation. Perhaps for an old man who has lived, whose energies are declining, it may be meditation.

People differ; there are many types of people. To someone who has a low kind of energy, sitting underneath a tree in a yoga posture may be the best meditation, because the yoga posture is the least energy-expensive—the least. When the spine is erect, making a ninety-degree angle with the earth, your body expends the least energy possible. If you are leaning toward the left or toward the front, then your body starts spending more energy, because the gravitation starts pulling you downwards and you have to keep yourself, you have to hold yourself so that you don't fall. This is expenditure. An erect spine was found to need the least spending of energy.

Then sitting with your hands together in the lap is also very very useful for low-energy people, because when both the hands are touching each other, your body electricity starts moving in a circle. It does not go out of your body; it becomes an inner circle, the energy moves inside you.

You must know that energy is always released through the fingers; energy is never released from round-shaped things. For example, your head cannot release energy; it contains it. Energy is released through the fingers, the toes of the feet, and the hands. In a certain yoga posture the feet are together, so one foot releases energy and it enters into the other foot; one hand releases energy and it enters into the other hand. You go on taking your own energy, you become an inner circle of energy. It is very resting, it is very relaxing.

The yoga posture is the most relaxed posture possible. It is more relaxing than even sleep, because when you are asleep your whole body is being pulled by gravitation. When you are horizontal it is relaxing in a totally different way. It is relaxing because it brings you back to the ancient days when man was an animal, horizontal. It is relaxing because it is regressive; it helps you to become an animal again.

That's why in a lying posture you cannot think clearly, it becomes difficult to think. Try it. You can dream easily but you cannot think easily; for thinking you have to sit. The more erect you sit, the better is the possibility to think. Thinking is a late arrival; when man became vertical, thinking arrived. When man used to be horizontal, dreaming was there but thinking was not. So when you lie down you start dreaming; thinking disappears. It is a kind of relaxation, because thinking stops; you regress.

The yoga posture is a good meditation for those who have low energy, for those who are ill, for those who are old, for those who have lived their whole life and now are coming closer and closer to death.

Thousands of Buddhist monks have died in the sitting lotus posture, because the best way to receive death is in the lotus posture—because in the lotus posture you will be fully alert, and because energies will be disappearing, they will be becoming less and less every moment. Death is coming. In a lotus posture you can keep alertness to the very end. And to be alert while you are dying is one of the greatest experiences, the ultimate in orgasm.

And if you are awake while you are dying you will have a totally different kind of birth: you will be born awake. One who dies awake is born awake. One who dies unconscious is born unconscious. One who dies with awareness can choose the right womb for himself; he has a choice, he has earned it. The man who dies unconsciously has no right to choose the womb; the womb happens unconsciously, accidentally.

The man who dies perfectly alert in this life will be coming only once more, because next time there will be no need to come. Just a little work is left: the other life will do that work. For one who is dying with awareness, only one thing is left now: he has had no time to radiate his awareness into compassion. Next time he can radiate his awareness into compassion. And unless awareness becomes compassion, something remains incomplete, something remains imperfect.

Running can be a meditation—jogging, dancing, swimming, anything can be a meditation. My definition of meditation is: whenever your body, mind, soul are functioning together in rhythm it is meditation, because it will bring the fourth in. And if you are alert that you are doing it as a meditation—not to take part in the Olympics, but doing it as a meditation—then it is tremendously beautiful . . .

But the basic fundamental is, whatever the meditation, it has to fill this requirement: that the body, mind, consciousness, all three should function in unity. Then suddenly one day the fourth has arrived: the witnessing. Or if you want to, call it God; call it God or nirvana or Tao or whatever you will.

YOU ARE NOT THE BODY

If one feels identified with the body one is always in a hurry, hence the Western hurriedness, hence the Western obsession with speed. Basically it is identification with the body. Life is running fast, going out of your hands—do something and do it instantly, and be in a hurry, otherwise you will miss it. And find better means of doing it, faster means of doing it. Speed has become a mania. How to reach some place with greater speed; that has become the sole concern. Why you want to reach there is nobody's concern. Why in the first place do you want to go there? That is not the point, but you should reach it faster. And the moment you reach there you start thinking of reaching somewhere else.

The mind remains in a constantly feverish state. This is basically because we have become identified with the periphery, and the body is going to die, so death haunts one. In the West death is still a taboo. One taboo has been broken—the taboo about sex—but the second taboo, which is deeper than the first, still exists. It needs some Freud again to break this taboo. People don't talk about death, or even if they do, they talk euphemistically—that the man has gone to God, to heaven, has gone to eternal rest. But if the man has only lived in the body, he has not gone anywhere. He is dead, simply dead—dust unto dust. And the one who has gone into another body was never here in this body, because he never became aware of it; the man remained completely oblivious of it.

The other way is to become alert about your inner consciousness. The body is heavy, very prominent, apparent, visible, touchable, tangible. The consciousness is not visible, not so much on the surface. One has to search for it, one has to dig deep. It needs effort, it needs a constant commitment to explore one's own being. It is a journey, but once you start feeling yourself as consciousness you live in a totally different world. Then there is no hurry because consciousness is eternal, and there is no worry because consciousness knows no disease, no death, no defeat. Then there is no need to search for anything else. The body lacks everything, hence it creates desires upon desires; the body is a beggar. But consciousness is an emperor—it possesses the whole world, it is the master.

Once you have known the face of your inner being, you become relaxed. Then life is no more a desire but a celebration. Then all is given already: the stars and the moon and the sun and the mountains and the rivers and the people—all is given. You have to start living it.

This has to become your exploration. This is what life is all about: an exploration into consciousness. It is there but it is a hidden treasure. And, naturally, when you have a treasure you keep it hidden deep down so nobody can steal it. God has put consciousness at the deepest core of your being. The body is just the porch; it is not the innermost chamber. But many people simply live in the porch and they think this is life; they never enter the house of their being.

Let life become a journey into your own self. Use the body, love the body—it is a beautiful mechanism, a precious gift, great are its mysteries—but don't become identified with it. The body is just like the airplane and you are the pilot. The airplane is beautiful and very useful, but the pilot is not the airplane and the pilot has to remember that he is distinct, distant, aloof, away, far away. He is the master of the vehicle.

So use the body as a vehicle but let consciousness be enthroned.

FROM GOAL SEEKER TO CELEBRATOR

Relaxation is a state of affairs where your energy is not moving anywhere, not to the future, not to the past—it is simply there with you. In the silent pool of your own energy, in the warmth of it, you are enveloped. This moment is all. There is no other moment. Time stops—then there is relaxation. If time is there, there is no relaxation. Simply, the clock stops; there is no time.

This moment is all. You don't ask for anything else; you simply enjoy it. Ordinary things can be enjoyed because they are beautiful. In fact, nothing is ordinary—if God exists, then everything is extraordinary.

Just small things . . . Walking on the lawn when the dewdrops have not evaporated yet, and just feeling totally there— the texture, the touch of the lawn, the coolness of the dewdrops, the morning wind, the sun rising. What more do you need to be happy? What more is possible to be happy? Just lying down in the night on the cool sheet on your bed, feeling the texture; feeling that the sheet is getting warmer and warmer, and you are shrouded in darkness, the silence of the night. With closed eyes you simply feel yourself. What more do you need? It is too much—a deep gratitude arises: this is relaxation.

Relaxation means this moment is more than enough, more than can be asked and expected. Nothing to ask, more than enough, than you can desire—then the energy never moves anywhere. It becomes a placid pool. In your own energy, you dissolve. This moment is relaxation. Relaxation is neither of the body nor of the mind, relaxation is of the total. That's why buddhas go on saying, "Become desireless," because they know that if there is desire, you cannot relax. They go on saying, "Bury the dead," because if you are too much concerned with the past, you cannot relax. They go on saying, "Enjoy this very moment."

Jesus says, "Look at the lilies. Consider the lilies in the field— they toil not and they are more beautiful, their splendor is greater than King Solomon. They are arrayed in more beautiful aroma than King Solomon ever was. Look, consider the lilies!"

What is he saying? He is saying, "Relax! You need not toil for it—in fact, everything is provided." Jesus says, "If he looks after the birds of air, animals, wild animals, trees and plants, then why are you worried? Will he not look after you?" This is relaxation. Why are you so much worried about the future? Consider the lilies, watch the lilies, and become like lilies—and then relax. Relaxation is not a posture; relaxation is a total transformation of your energy.

Energy can have two dimensions. One is motivated, going somewhere, a goal somewhere; this moment is only a means and the goal is somewhere else to be achieved. This is one dimension of your energy, this is the dimension of activity, goal-oriented. Then everything is a means; somehow it has to be done and you have to reach to the goal, then you will relax. But for this type of energy the goal never comes, because this type of energy goes on changing every present moment into a means for something else, into the future. The goal always remains on the horizon. You go on running, but the distance remains the same.

No, there is another dimension of energy: that dimension is unmotivated celebration. The goal is here, now; the goal is not somewhere else. In fact, you are the goal. In fact, there is no other fulfillment than of this moment—consider the lilies. When you are the goal and when the goal is not in the future, when there is nothing to be achieved, rather, you have just to celebrate it, you have already achieved it, it is there. This is relaxation, unmotivated energy.

So, to me, there are two types of persons: the goal-seekers and the celebrators. The goal-oriented, they are the mad ones; they are going, by and by, crazy, and they are creating their own craziness. And then the craziness has its own momentum: by and by, they move deeper into it—then they are completely lost. The other type of person is not a goal-seeker—he is not a seeker at all, he is a celebrator.

And this I teach to you: Be the celebrators, celebrate! Already there is too much: the flowers have bloomed, the birds are singing, the sun is there in the sky—celebrate it! You are breathing and you are alive, and you have consciousness—celebrate it! Then suddenly you relax, then there is no tension, then there is no anguish. The whole energy that becomes anguish becomes gratitude; your whole heart goes on beating with a deep thankfulness—that is prayer. That's all prayer is about: a heart beating with a deep thankfulness.

No need to do anything for it. Just understand the movement of the energy, the unmotivated movement of the energy. It flows, but not toward a goal, it flows as a celebration. It moves, not toward a goal, it moves because of its own overflowing energy.

A child is dancing and jumping and running around; ask him, "Where are you going?" He is not going anywhere—you will look foolish to him. Children always think that adults are foolish. What a nonsensical question, "Where are you going?" Is there any need to go anywhere? A child simply cannot answer your question because it is irrelevant. He is not going anywhere. He will simply shrug his shoulders. He will say, "Nowhere." Then the goal-oriented mind asks, "Then why are you running?"—because to us an activity is relevant only when it leads somewhere.

And I tell you, there is nowhere to go: here is all. The whole existence culminates in this moment, it converges into this moment. The whole existence is pouring already in this moment; all that is there is pouring into this moment—it is here, now. A child is simply enjoying the energy. He has too much. He is running, not because he has to reach somewhere, but because he has too much; he has to run.

Act unmotivated, just an overflow of your energy. Share, but don't trade; don't make bargains. Give because you have; don't give to take back—because then you will be in misery. All traders go to hell. If you want to find the greatest traders and bargainers, go to hell; you will find them there. Heaven is not for traders. Heaven is for celebrators.

What is to be practiced then? To be more and more at ease. To be more and more here and now. To be more and more in action, and less and less in activity. To be more and more hollow, empty, passive. To be more and more a watcher—indifferent, not expecting anything, not desiring anything. To be happy with yourself as you are. To be celebrating.

REMEMBER THE RESIDENT

Man is in the body but is not the body. The body is beautiful, the body has to be loved and respected, but one has not to forget that one is not it, that one is a resident in the body. The body is a temple: it is a host to you but you are not part of it. The body is a contribution from the earth; you come from the sky. In you, as in every embodied being, the earth and the sky are meeting: it is a love affair of earth and sky.

The moment you die, nothing dies; it only appears that it does to others from the outside. The body falls back into the earth to have a little rest and the soul falls back into the sky to have a little rest. Again and again the meeting will happen; in millions of forms the play will continue. It is an eternal occurrence.

But one can get too identified with the body; that creates misery. If one starts feeling "I am the body" then life becomes very heavy. Then small things disturb, small pains are too much: just a little hurt and one is disturbed and disoriented.

A little distance is needed between you and your body. That distance is created by being aware of the fact "I am not the body, I cannot be the body. I am conscious of it, so it is an object of my consciousness, and whatever is an object of my consciousness cannot be my consciousness. The consciousness is watching, witnessing, and whatever is witnessed is separate."

As this experience deepens in you, miseries start disappearing and evaporating. Then pain and pleasure are almost alike, then success and failure are the same, then life and death are not different. Then one has no choice, one lives in a cool choicelessness. In that cool choicelessness God descends. That has been the search of all religions, that cool choicelessness. In India we call it samadhi, in Japan they call it satori; Christian mystics have called it ecstasy.

The word "ecstasy" is very significant; it means standing out. Standing out of your own body, knowing that you are separate, is the meaning of ecstasy. And the moment it happens you are part of the lost paradise again, paradise is regained.

CHAPTER SEVEN

Reminding Yourself of the Forgotten Language of Talking to the BodyMind— An OSHO Meditative Therapy

"People need to be taught how to
make friends with the body."

This guided meditation is a process of being reminded of a language most of us have forgotten. It's the language of communicating with your own body. Communicating with the body, talking to it, listening to its messages has been a well known practice in ancient Tibet.

Modern medical science is only now beginning to recognize what the sages and mystics have always known: that the mind and body are not separate entities but deeply related. The mind can affect the condition of the body, just as the condition of the body can affect the mind.

Osho has created many meditation techniques especially for today's men and women.

This guided meditation of talking to the mind and body has been developed with his guidance. He says:

Once you start communicating with your body, *things become very easy. The body need not be forced, it can be persuaded. One need not fight with the body—that's ugly, violent, aggressive, and any sort of conflict is going to create more and more tension. So you need not* *be in any conflict—let comfort be the rule. And the body is such a beautiful gift from God that to fight with it is to deny God himself. It is a shrine . . . we are enshrined in it; it is a temple. We exist in it and we have to take every care of it—it is our responsibility.*

So for seven days . . . It will look a little absurd in the beginning because we have never been taught to talk to our own body—and miracles can happen through it. They are already happening without our knowing it. When I am saying something to you, my hand follows in a gesture. I am talking to you—it is my mind that is communicating something to you. My body is following it. The body is in rapport with the mind.

When you want to raise the hand, you have to do nothing—you simply raise it. Just the very idea that you want to raise it and the body follows it; it is a miracle. In fact, biology or physiology has not yet been able to explain how it happens. Because an idea is an idea; you want to raise your hand—it is an idea. How does this idea become transformed into a physical message to the hand? And it does not take any time at all—in a split second; sometimes without any time gap.

For example, I am talking to you and my hand will go on collaborating; there is no time gap. It is as if the body is running parallel to the mind. It is very sensitive—one should learn how to talk to the body, and many things can be done.

—Osho

HOW TO USE THE CD

This meditation is about making friends with yourself, with your body, and also with your mind. You will become aware of how your mind, its thoughts and feelings, express themselves through your body. Pain, diseases, addictions (e.g., eating too much, alcohol, sugar, etc.) will be dealt with and can be healed.

This process is a chance to mobilize your self-healing energies and to relax deeply.

The meditation has three parts:

1. You will be speaking to specific parts of your body, and to your whole body.

   It is a good idea to speak aloud as this will help you to stay alert and conscious.

2. You will be communicating with your unconscious mind about a problem that you may be having with your body, whether it is a question of being sick, being overweight, being in pain, etc., or simply wishing to feel more alive and healthy.

   In a deeply relaxed state you will connect with the part of your unconscious mind that is responsible for the condition of your body, approaching it with respect and friendliness. For example, if you experience your weight as a problem, the part of your unconscious mind responsible for this is a very devoted servant to you, and a guardian. By making you overweight this guardian has been trying to help and protect you. In a deep trance state, the guardian can create new ways to fulfill its positive intention while allowing your body to be natural and healthy again. In this way you arrive at a new understanding about your body-mind mechanism and its ability to heal itself.

3. A healing trance, deepening the understanding that your body, your mind, and your soul are one.

Before you begin to use the technique, however, a few important points:

FIRST:

It is important to remember that **pain and other recurring symptoms of physical discomfort can be an indication of serious illness.** This technique is offered with the assumption that you have consulted your doctor to determine whether or not this is the case.

SECOND:

Osho says that **this technique of talking to your mind and body can be used for anything that the body can already do, something that is within its ability.** If you ask the body to do something that is impossible, then the trust will be destroyed and it won't work. If you don't have eyes, he says, how can the body be told to see? But for ordinary things, like migraines and bodily pains and other functions that are within the capacity of the body to heal by itself, then this method can do much to help.

THIRD:

Don't talk directly to the discomfort or disease. The disease is not part of the organism, it is something external, in fact something *against* the organism. You must talk to the brain/body, not to the discomfort itself. And when it is gone, thank the brain and body for letting the discomfort go. Basically, we are talking to the brain and the brain talks to the body, but we don't know the language. We know that if we tell the arm to rise, we can raise it; it follows the instructions of the mind. But for the inner workings of the body/mind, we do not know exactly what the right instruction is so that the body will follow. Osho says, "This is the real trinity—the soul, the mind, and the body. The soul can do nothing directly; it is the one asking for the pain to go. The brain has to speak to the body."

Osho has given the following suggestions to people experimenting with the meditation, which may be helpful to you:

WEIGHT LOSS: "First tell the brain that you are sending a message to the body, and that the brain should pass it on. Then simply tell the body that five pounds or kilos less will be ideal and that you digest normally. Do not involve the eating at all. Just tell the body that some pounds less are needed. And when you get there, tell the body to stay there, that there is no need to lose any more weight or to gain more weight."

MIGRAINE: "Speak to the body in two ways. First speak to the whole body, telling it that its help is needed to send away this pain in the brain. Explain to the body that pain is not its natural way. There is no need to be carrying this pain. Then speak to the brain directly, in your own words telling it, 'I do love you but this pain is not part of your nature, and it is time to get rid of it.' And when it is gone simply remind the brain not to take it back."

PREPARING FOR THE MEDITATION

Becoming your own best friend is the deepest learning of this healing meditation.

So before you start the meditation make whatever arrangements are needed so that you will not be disturbed for the next hour, allowing yourself to relax deeply into this process.

Have a blanket nearby, so you can use it to be warm enough if you need it.

Take a few minutes to think about what issue or symptom of your body you would like to work with today. Then make yourself completely comfortable, however feels best for you, and turn on the CD. You have nothing else to do.

For more information about this process and Osho:

www.osho.com

This body awareness process is offered at the Osho Meditation Resort and in many places around the world as a program course. The process is usually offered for one hour per day over seven days. For detailed program information check: www.osho.com/bodymindbalancing

OSHO® MEDITATION RESORT

The Osho Meditation Resort is a place where people can have a direct personal experience of a new way of living with more alertness, relaxation, and fun. Located about 100 miles southeast of Mumbai in Pune, India, the resort offers a variety of programs to thousands of people who visit each year from more than a hundred countries around the world. www.osho.com/resort

ABOUT THE AUTHOR

Osho's teachings defy categorization, covering everything from the individual quest for meaning to the most urgent social and political issues facing society today. His books are not written but are transcribed from audio and video recordings of extemporaneous talks given to international audiences over a period of thirty-five years. Osho has been described by the *Sunday Times* in London as one of the "1000 Makers of the 20th Century" and by American author Tom Robbins as "the most dangerous man since Jesus Christ."

About his own work Osho has said that he is helping to create the conditions for the birth of a new kind of human being. He has often characterized this new human being as "Zorba the Buddha"—capable both of enjoying the earthy pleasures of a Zorba the Greek and the silent serenity of a Gautam Buddha. Running like a thread through all aspects of Osho's work is a vision that encompasses both the timeless wisdom of the East and the highest potential of Western science and technology.

Osho is also known for his revolutionary contribution to the science of inner transformation, with an approach to meditation that acknowledges the accelerated pace of contemporary life. His unique "Active Meditations" are designed to first release the accumulated stresses of body and mind, so that it is easier to experience the thought-free and relaxed state of meditation.

The voice heard on the guided meditation CD, "Reminding Yourself of the Forgotten Language of Talking to the BodyMind" belongs to Anando Hefley. A former lawyer and business magazine publisher, she understands well the tensions and stresses involved in everyday life. Having worked closely with Osho for many years, she brings sensitivity and enthusiasm to learning the knack of meditation. Anando has been practicing and teaching meditation and transformation workshops for more than twenty years, and conducts "Talking to the Body" workshops and trainings regularly at the Osho Meditation Resort in India and around the world.

OSHO®

LOOK WITHIN...

PHARMACY FOR THE SOUL

A comprehensive collection of meditations, relaxation and awareness exercises, and other practices for physical and emotional well-being.

0-312-32076-0   Paperback $11.95/$17.95 Can.
5 1/2" x 8 1/4"

MEDITATION: THE FIRST AND LAST FREEDOM

A practical guide to integrating meditation into all aspects of daily life, which includes instructions for over 60 meditation techniques, including the revolutionary Osho Active Meditations™.

0-312-33663-2   Paperback $12.95/$18.95 Can.
5" x 7 1/2"

INSIGHTS FOR A NEW WAY OF LIVING SERIES

The work of OSHO is about breaking free of the belief systems, attitudes, and prejudices that keep us from living life to the fullest. The Insights for a New Way of Living Series celebrates the unique individual that lives inside each human being, and challenges us to honor and be true to ourselves.

0-312-27563-3
$11.95/$17.95 Can.

0-312-20517-1
$11.95/$18.99 Can.

0-312-20519-8
$11.95/$18.99 Can.

0-312-32072-8
$11.95/$17.99 Can.

0-312-32070-1
$11.95/$17.95 Can.

0-312-27566-8
$11.95/$17.95 Can.

0-312-27567-6
$11.95/$17.95 Can.

0-312-32074-4
$11.95/$17.95 Can.

0-312-20561-9
$11.95/$17.95 Can.

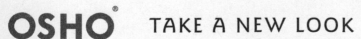

OSHO® TAKE A NEW LOOK www.OSHO.co

Osho is a registered trademark of Osho International Foundation.

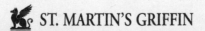

ST. MARTIN'S GRIFFIN